CLAN MACFAR...

A HISTOR...

CLAN MACFARLANE

A HISTORY

Angus MacFarlane

Angus MacFarlane, the third son of a Reading doctor, read theology at Oxford and spent his working life as a Vicar in both town and country parishes. Genealogical researches led him to friendship with the author of Clan MacFarlane's first history. His two previously published books were *The First Hundred Years – The Story of St Mary's Bromley Kent* and *Sandhill Park – A Story of Caring*, the history of a mental handicap hospital where he was chaplain.

Angus MacFarlane is married with two sons and two daughters. He lives in retirement in Blue Anchor, Somerset.

British Library Cataloguing in Publication Data
A catalogue record of this book is available from the British Library

ISBN 1 899863 57 5

First published 2001
by House of Lochar

Typeset by XL Publishing Services, Tiverton
Printed in Great Britain
by SRP Ltd, Exeter
for House of Lochar
Isle of Colonsay, Argyll PA61 7YR

FOR MY FAMILY
AND ESPECIALLY FOR MY BELOVED WIFE
HEATHER MARY

Acknowledgements

In their search for the history of their Clan, MacFarlanes will always owe their greatest debt to James MacFarlane who pioneered the work in his *History of Clan MacFarlane*, published in 1922 by David J. Clarke of Glasgow.

My aim has been to try to explain the wider context of the history of the Clan. Although I have not been able to check all the primary sources, I have used some of the quotations from this earlier book because they greatly enrich the text and I am grateful for them.

I must thank Ronald MacFarlane OBE, the son of the author James MacFarlane, for his constant support and encouragement.

I am deeply indebted to Mrs Mary Copp and Mrs Pat Abbott for their generous sharing of their typing and manuscript-reading skills.

For any errors I must accept full responsibility. It is inevitable in a work of this nature that there will be some and I apologise for them.

Angus MacFarlane
March 2000

Contents

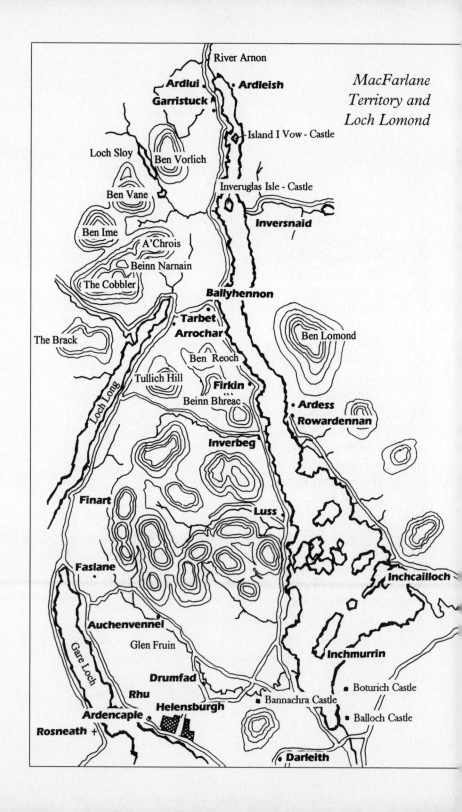

I

Beginnings

We learn from the Roman historian Tacitus that, before his father-in-law Agricola came to North Britain as the military governor in AD 81 with the 9th Legion, there were twenty-one tribes in the area. Thirteen of them lived in what is now known as the Highlands, called at that time by the Romans, 'Caledonia'.

The social life of these tribes could be described as that of Bronze Age Culture with some Iron Age features. Their homes, which were sometimes surrounded by a protective ditch, were made of turf and skins, and their main defence a hill fort. They conducted their warfare with spears, bows and arrows, broadswords, axes and daggers, supported on occasion with disorganised chariot charges. Of their home life all that can certainly be said is that it must have been very primitive, with the struggle for food being their main anxiety and occupation. There was milk, flesh from their flocks and their hunting and, later on, with the decline of Druidic influence which had superstitions about it, fish. Although they wore practically no clothing they enjoyed having ornaments such as necklaces, bracelets, finger and ear rings. From the Druidical monuments that remain the presumption is that their religion was some kind of Druidism, but it is much disputed as to how developed it was. Its strength seems to have been more in the realms of social life and of thought – unlike some other places where it was both politically and militarily significant.

Fighters of courage though these tribes proved to be, they rarely thought of combining together for any length of time to repel a common enemy. They did, however, do this briefly when confronted by the Roman general, Agricola. Somewhere between the Firth of Tay and the Firth of Moray at Mons Graupius, under the leadership of Calgacus they fought and were defeated by the Roman Army in AD 83. The discovery of a Roman camp at Durno in Aberdeenshire has led some to identify Mons Graupius with the mountain Bennachie. The Romans claimed that their own losses amounted to three hundred and sixty, with the British sustaining a loss of ten thousand. As they put the British forces at thirty thousand before the battle, this would mean that twenty thousand of their enemies lived to fight another day.

This they did by continually making attacks on the Roman camps. Agricola then built a defensive line of forts from the Forth to the Clyde. He was unable to execute any further defensive plans as he was suddenly recalled to Rome. In AD 121, for greater security, Hadrian, who was now in charge, built the wall still known by his name between the Solway Firth and the River Tyne; that is, between Old Kirkpatrick and Carridon. Later, Lollius Urbicus drove the tribes back to Agricola's original line which he then strengthened by joining up the forts with a wall some thirty-six miles long, now known as the Antonine Wall.

With the decline of Roman power due to the withdrawal of Roman forces in AD 407 to meet the increasing pressure of Barbarian invasions nearer home, North Britain became more and more vulnerable to foreign invasions. There came the Picts, who occupied territory from the Forth to the Pentland Firth, and the Scots, a warlike tribe from Northern Ireland, who held Argyllshire and the neighbouring islands, ultimately establishing their kingdom of Dalraida with its capital at the Castle of Dunadd. This kingdom lasted from AD 500–800. There came, too, the Britons who held the valley of the Clyde and Strathclyde, and also the Angles who originated in Schleswig and set up their kingdom from the River Tees to the Firth of Forth.

By about one hundred and fifty years after the withdrawal of the Romans there were no longer thirteen tribes, for they had now been absorbed into one or other of these four kingdoms. Over the years each kingdom rose and fell in power, but gradually they were brought together into one.

The unification was achieved mainly by fighting, but it was also greatly helped by Christian missionaries whose work slowly brought the people under one religious banner, instead of being some Christian, some Druidic, and some pagan. Among the missionary pioneers of the time were Ninian (c.432), working among the South Picts in the Strathclyde region; Columba (c.521–597), based on Iona and working among the Picts; Kentigern (Mungo), a member of the Pictish royal family, evangelised among the Britons in the Glasgow area; and Aidan, who founded the Lindisfarne community and worked among the Angles, dying in 651.

The military muscle for the unification was supplied chiefly by Kenneth MacAlpine (843–860) and Malcolm II (1005–1034), and resulted in the triumph of the Scottish kingdom. Until this happened, the divisions between the four kingdoms weakened their opposition to the Norsemen, who from the end of the eighth century had been so successfully invading North Britain that, in the course of one hundred years, they had conquered and taken possession of the Western Isles, Sutherland, Caithness, Orkney and Shetland.

Duncan's son, Malcolm III (1057–1093), although he was married to the saintly Margaret, Edward the Confessor's sister, was a ferocious warrior. Margaret had come to Scotland as a refugee after William the Conqueror's success in 1066, so Malcolm's sympathies were with the English rather than the Normans. Nevertheless, when in 1072 William came with a powerful army to claim the overlordship of Scotland, Malcolm wisely accepted the situation and paid homage to him at Abernethy in Perthshire. Whether he did this for all Scotland, or just for Cumbria and Lothian, was a much disputed question.

From now on, in the matter of the possession of land, tribal claims had to make way for the Feudal System – a change that meant that land came to be held not by tribal custom but by a charter granted by the King to lords, and nobles for services rendered. It was this change in the system of land ownership that led to so many blood-thirsty and cruel episodes in Scottish history, as some supported and others opposed the changes.

II
William, the Lion

The territory of the Levanach, which comprised much of present-day Dunbartonshire, belonged originally to the Celtic tribe known as the Attacotti and, as we have already seen, was later overrun and incorporated into the kingdom established by the Dalriadic Scots from Northern Ireland.

Dunbartonshire occupies some two hundred and sixty-seven square miles. It is defined by Loch Lomond to the east, Loch Long to the west, and the estuary of the Clyde to the south. Generally it is mountainous country, its highest peak being Ben Vorlich at 3092 feet. With its mountains, lochs, trees and grandeur, it is almost commonplace that those who come to the area should wax lyrical about the scenery, the more so if they are touched by romantic notions of its history. This is well illustrated by the words of Mr George Eyre-Todd who was referring in particular to that area of Dunbartonshire that became part of the MacFarlane heritage. The words are quoted in MacFarlane's 1922 history:

> One of the loveliest regions in the West Highlands is the district about the head of Loch Long and Loch Lomond, which was for some five centuries the patrimony of the chiefs of the MacFarlane clan. With the waves of one of the most beautiful sea lochs of the Clyde rippling far into its recesses, and the tideless waters of the Queen of Scottish lochs sleeping under the birch-clad slopes on another side, while high among its fastnesses, between the towering heights of Ben Arthur and Ben Voirlich, shimmers in a silver lane the jewel-like Loch Sloy, this ancient territory could not but, in the course of centuries,

5

produce a race of men instinct with the love of the mountains and the moors, and with all the chivalrous qualities which go to make the traditional character of the Highlanders of Scotland. This is nothing less than fact in the case of Clan Farlan.

In the early part of the thirteenth century the Chief recorded in this area is 'Aluin de Levanax'. Although there is no evidence to support the view, it should be noted that some antiquaries believe that this leading family is descended from a Northumbrian named Archillus who escaped from there to Scotland in the face of William the Conqueror's advance. Another tradition holds that the family was of native origin. Yet another tradition claims that this family were hereditary holders of the offices of seneschal (or overseer/ historian) of the royal households of Strathern, and baillie of the Abthanery of Dull in Perthshire. These responsibilities thus included the management of a large household, and some degree of administration of justice.

The first-named of the holders of these offices, and who ranked as a mormaer (or baron) of the Levanach, was Malduin. By about 1180 the Chief of the Levanach was Archill and he was raised by his king, William I, to be the first Earl of Lennox. For elevation to such a dignity he must have served his king in some notable capacity, and King William I's reign, marked as it was with frequent rebellions and disturbances, provided many such opportunities.

King William, 'the Lion', was a grandson of the great King David of Scotland and he came to the throne in 1165 to reign both as a free king and then as a vassal king until 1214.

William's brother Malcolm IV, whom he succeeded, ruled from 1153 to 1165 and, because of his youthful appearance, was known as 'the Maiden'. He was only twelve years old when he came to the throne and, although he disputed the ownership of the territories of Northumberland and Cumberland with Henry II of England, in view of his age, together with the troubles he encountered in his own kingdom, he thought it wiser to cede these areas to Henry.

However, when William came to the throne he determined to win them back again. In 1174 he led his forces into England and beseiged Alnwick. Unfortunately for him, and for Scotland, he was surprised by the English in a fog, and when his horse was killed under him he was captured and imprisoned in Falaise in Normandy. This humbling and bitter experience for one who had adopted the rampant lion as his heraldic device – still associated with Scotland – was made worse when he secured his release only by recognising Henry as his feudal overlord and by seeing English soldiers installed in castles at Edinburgh, Stirling, Roxburgh, Jedburgh, Berwick and Aberdeen.

These troubles were galling enough, but throughout his reign he also had to cope with rebellious barons. In 1187 a revolt took place in Ross-shire which he settled for a time by setting up garrisons. Later, a Donal Bane with the support of the Lord of Galloway made an unsuccessful attempt to win the crown, being defeated with five hundred of his followers and killed on Mangarty Moor. The King was out in arms again in 1196, this time against Harold, Earl of Orkney and Caithness. The Earl was defeated but his son, Torphin, continued the struggle until he too was beaten in battle and ended his days in prison. His punishment took the traditional form of splitting up the family lands and giving them to others. There was yet another rebellion in 1211, also in Ross, this time led by Donal Bane's son, Guthred. After much fighting Guthred was defeated, caught and executed.

Castles set up at Aberdeen, Ayr, Larne, Dumfries, Dunkeith and Redcastle are evidence of William's efforts to keep his land in order. The King's reign should be remembered, too, for his founding of the impressive Cluniac Abbey at Arbroath which flourished until as late as 1606. Here he was eventually laid to rest. He was also the creator of several Royal Burghs. Perhaps, too, it should be noted that during his time there was a great increase in commerce, particularly in wool, skins and fish. Berwick became Scotland's most prosperous town.

Henry II of England was succeeded by Richard Coeur de Lion who, in his enthusiasm for the Crusades, needed all the money he could raise. He therefore accepted ten thousand marks from King William in 1189 as the purchase price of his status as a free king.

This then was the king who created the first Earl of Lennox. How much the Earl was involved in all this military activity is not clear, but he must have been to some degree, so proving worthy of recognition. As we shall see, it is from the Earls of Lennox that the MacFarlanes trace their origin, and from whom they originally received the charters for their lands.

Loch Sloy

III

The First Chief

Of Dumbarton Rock it has been said that it has a longer recorded history as a stronghold than any other place in Britain. The name itself means 'the fortress of the Britons.' From the castle on the Rock King Duncan ruled over the Kingdom of Strathclyde until it was incorporated into the Kingdom of the Scots in 1034. The castle retained its royal status because it was a place of strategic importance, even when political power was centred elsewhere. In a charter of 1238 we see that this castle became the home of Malduin, third Earl of Lennox, while still remaining the property of the King. At this time it would have been the childhood home of Malduin's younger brother Gilchrist, who was to become the first Chief of Clan MacFarlane.

From 1214 until 1249, Alexander II, the son of William the Lion, was King of Scotland and, like his father, had problems to resolve in some of the remoter parts of his kingdom. There were rebellions in Galloway which took several efforts to subdue. The people of Argyll thought it safe to pay little attention to their king's requirements and so, in 1222, he set out with an army to teach them otherwise. The people of Caithness also had to be disciplined and to reckon with their king for killing their bishop, even though it was his greediness over the matter of tithes that had provoked them. It is probable that Alwyn, the second Earl of Lennox, was involved in the support of his king in some of these events.

Before he died in 1225, Alwyn had become the father of eight sons, only two of whom left male descendants. The eldest son, Malduin, became the third Earl, who

9

subsequently had to hand over the castle to the King. The fifth son, Aulay, was created heritable Baillie of the Lennox, and the eighth son, Corc, was ancestor of Leckie of that Ilk.

We are particularly concerned with the fourth son, Gilchrist. He is reckoned by most historians to have been the first Chief of Clan MacFarlane, because it was he who received the first charter for the lands which for six hundred years made up the main estate of the clan. Later, as sons of the chiefs moved away from the home estate there were perhaps as many as six other large estates. There were large houses at Inversnaid, Ardess, Gartartan, the Mains of Kilmaronock, Ballagan, Campsie, Drumfad and Auchinvenal. Indeed, graveyards in Aberfoyle, Gartmore, Balmaha, Inchailloch, Luss and Tarbet give evidence of the presence of MacFarlanes in many other places in the region.

However, the main estate of some thirty-one thousand acres was at Arrochar, and it was the charter to this territory that Gilchrist received from his brother, Earl Malduin, probably in 1225 when Malduin succeeded to the title. Its contents are known from later charters. The library of The Royal Faculty of Advocates in Glasgow contains some one hundred and ten charters and other papers relating to the Arrochar MacFarlanes. One charter there is dated 1395, and another 1430. In translation, one such document describes the MacFarlane territory as:

> The lands of Upper Arrochar down from Luss, lying between the small brooks which are called Aldyvach and Oldquchulin on one side and the small brooks which are called Hernan Hings and Trostan on the other side, together with the Islands of Elanvow, Elanvanow, Elanrouglas and Elaig.

Thus this beautiful and magnificent territory became the home land, by charter, of Gilchrist and his successors, and so it remained for six hundred years. In many subsequent charters he is known as Arrochar McGilchrist. His name appears as witness on other charters than his own; in

10

particular, on one dated 1225, relating to the Island of Clare-Inch in Loch Lomond and, on another dated 1238, referring to land in Baldernock.

Gilchrist's king, Alexander II, in addition to having to deal with several small insurrections, was faced with the major problem that the Lord of Argyll paid homage not to him, but to the King of Norway. Alexander determined to enforce this tribute to himself. He set off with his forces into Argyll and at once the Lord of Argyll appealed to the King of Norway for help. However, as Alexander died while advancing and before the matter had been settled, it fell to his son, Alexander III (1249–1286), to assert his claim. So it came about that in 1263 there took place an event, forever recorded in Scotland's history, which deeply concerned the MacFarlanes. It became known as Haco's Foray.

Haakon, King of Norway, decided to settle once and for all his claim to Scottish lands in his possession, so he set out with over one hundred ships. Forty of these landed at the head of Loch Long in the very heart of MacFarlane territory. A fierce battle took place at a spot known as Ballyhennon in which the men of Arrochar were defeated. There is a noticeable mound in the field where this battle is believed to have been fought, although now there is a hedge running through part of it. Tradition believes that the burial ground at Ballyhennon contains the bodies of the Arrochar men who fell, and that two small mounds in the grounds of Arrochar House cover the fallen of their enemies. It is believed that, for safety, Gilchrist put his family in a stronghold somewhere above Arrochar. Was this, we wonder, somewhere up Glen Loin on the way to Loch Sloy? The enemy would have ventured up that route at great risk, and in fact we know from history that, following their usual practice, they proceeded to pillage the countryside around the loch. They then dragged some ships along the mile-long strip of land over to Loch Lomond, continuing to plunder, kill and destroy as they went and then pursued their commando-like incursion deep into Dunbartonshire and Stirlingshire.

Eventually the victors returned with all their booty to their ships in Loch Long. They must have set sail in good heart, but they were unfortunate enough to be hit by a three-day storm which destroyed many of their ships. The end of the story came for them when their reduced forces clashed with Alexander's army at the Battle of Largs in 1263. They were so utterly defeated that Norway's kings could no longer sustain their claims to sovereignty over Scottish territories.

Gilchrist, Chief of MacFarlane, must have been involved in all this conflict in his own territory – indeed, at its very centre. No doubt, he was supported by his immediate feudal overlords, the third and fourth Lennox Earls, Malduin and Malcolm.

Ruins of Inveruglas Castle

IV
A Signature

The second Chief of Clan MacFarlane was Gilchrist's son, Duncan (1284–1296). He received the charter confirming his lands from his cousin Malcolm, the fourth Earl of Lennox, whose daughter, Matilda, he married. The date of the charter, in which he is called McGilchrist, must have been before 1284 and, although we do not know anything about the witnesses to it, at least their names are recorded as 'Simon Flandreuse, Master Duncan, son of Amelick, Master Henry of Ventere Ponte and Malcolm of Drumeth.' The Chief himself appears as a witness to a charter granted by the Earl to Michael M'Kessan, relating to lands at Garchell and Ballat.

Duncan lived in a particularly unsettled period of Scottish history. When Alexander III died in 1286 his grand-daughter, Margaret, was heir to the throne and only three years old. Her mother, Alexander's daughter, had married Eric, King of Norway, and Margaret had been born in that country. Because of her tender age six guardians were appointed to look after Scotland's affairs. Inevitably people began to wonder who would succeed to the throne should anything happen to Margaret.

Robert Bruce, the son of William the Lion's nephew David, collected together an army thinking it to be a propitious moment to try to win the crown for himself. However, most people, especially some of the barons, did not want him, preferring to have Margaret. The King of Norway then asked Edward I of England to make sure that no one but the rightful heir should sit on Scotland's throne. Edward readily agreed to do this for he planned that his own son, Edward, should marry Margaret. Sadly, Margaret died in 1290 on the ship bringing her from Norway.

This tragic event led at once to thirteen claimants putting themselves forward for the crown, three of whom were descended from the great King David I. To avoid civil war, the leaders in Scotland asked Edward to settle the issue. Rejecting Bruce, who had the stronger claim, he chose John Balliol, perhaps thinking that he could more easily manipulate him than any of the others towards strengthening his own claims to feudal sovereignty. In fact, having chosen him he then tried to exert his authority by ordering Balliol to raise forces and money to help him in his war against France. Ignoring this demand, Balliol completely repudiated Edward by making a treaty with France. Edward decided upon a fierce punishment. He ruthlessly destroyed Berwick, at that time a prosperous Scottish town, and then reinforced his message by inflicting the same fate on Dunbar. After the Battle of Dunbar and the fall of the castles at Edinburgh, Roxburgh and Stirling, Balliol had to submit.

Edward then determined to ensure that he was recognised as Lord of Scotland. English garrisons were established, English judges handled the law, and English tax-collectors carried out their unpopular task. As it was of vital significance in the enthroning of Scottish kings, he removed the Stone of Scone to Westminster, and then unequivocally enforced the recognition of his claims by compelling all who held land in Scotland to sign a list recognising him as their king. This list of some two thousand names is known as 'The Ragman's Roll' from the ribbons with the signatories' seals on them. It was signed in 1296 and, for the Scots, was a humiliating document. Among the names on this list may be seen the signature of Duncan, second Chief of Clan MacFarlane, who is described as 'son of Gilchrist of Levanax.'

Whatever these signatures meant they did not mean that the spirit of Scottish nationalism was broken. Indeed, there were vast areas, particularly in the Highlands, into which

English power had not penetrated and, when William
Wallace set out to free his country from the English, it was
not long before large numbers rallied round him. He started
off with great success capturing towns and castles, drawing
more and more support as he went. His success led to a
confrontation at Stirling Bridge where the English, under the
leadership of the Earl of Surrey, were defeated. It was a short-
lived victory for the next year, in 1298, Wallace was defeated
by Edward at the Battle of Falkirk. He managed to evade
capture for some seven years, but then it is believed that he
was betrayed by Sir John Monteith and taken to London for
a cruel execution.

The Chief's signature alone shows that Duncan was unable
to avoid being drawn into the wider affairs of the nation before
the chieftainship passed into the hands of his son, Malduin,
in 1296.

Upper Uglas

V

For His Country

Within a year of the death of William Wallace there arose
another great hero of Scottish history, Robert Bruce,
Earl of Carrick and Lord Annandale. He was the grandson
of the Bruce whose claim to the throne after the death of
Alexander III had been rejected by Edward I. As a landowner
in England as well as in Scotland, Bruce sometimes supported
Edward in his campaigns but he had, nevertheless, ambitions
towards the Scottish throne.

Most of the nobles were against his personal aims,
remembering, perhaps with jealousy, the claims made by his
grandfather. His particular rivals were the Balliols and Sir
John Comyn (Red Comyn). As a result of a heated quarrel
in church at Dumfries, Bruce killed Sir John and made yet
more enemies of the powerful MacDougalls, who were
relatives of Sir John. In a decisive step towards winning the
kingdom, Bruce went ahead and engineered his own
coronation at Scone in the presence of a few distinguished
people. He still, however, had to secure power and the
struggle was not going to be an easy one.

In 1306 at Methven near Perth, being surprised by an
English force, he lost the ensuing battle. For some time he
and his followers wandered about the Highlands evading his
enemies. Arriving at Tyndrum, near Glen Falloch, on his way
to Kintyre, he was attacked by the MacDougalls and only
just managed to escape. Coming down Glen Falloch he and
his party found themselves on the east rather than the west
side of Loch Lomond. Eventually they found a small boat
which ferried them two at a time to the other side.

Unexpectedly, Malcolm the 5th Earl of Lennox met them in his territory – or, more precisely, on MacFarlane land. Bruce and his men were given generous hospitality and helped on their way.

Three miles south of Tarbet, at a place called Firkin, there is a tree known as Bruce's tree, where some believed that he waited while the ferrying took place. The 'Friends of Loch Lomond' secured its survival when it was threatened by a new road project. There is also in the beautiful Glen Loin a cave known as Bruce's Cave, which is large enough to shelter about fifty men. The exact crossing place is impossible to identify, but the cave is certainly in the glen whether it was so used by Bruce or not.

After the death of Edward I, Bruce, knowing that Edward II had too much on his mind at home to worry very much about Scotland, took his opportunity. Gradually the English were driven out of one place after another – Edinburgh, Perth, Linlithgow, Roxburgh, and many others in Galloway – until the strategically important Stirling Castle itself came under threat. Edward now came with a strong army in 1314. The fierce and famous battle of Bannockburn resolved the issue when the Scots, outnumbered by three to one, won the field and Edward himself only just managed to escape.

The chiefs involved in this fight for Scotland's freedom are firmly recorded. The named chiefs were M'Kay, Mackintosh, Macpherson, Cameron, Sinclair, Campbell, Menzies, Maclean, Sutherland, Robertson, Grant, Fraser, Mac-Farlane, Ross, MacGregor, Munro, Mackenzie and Macquarrie. They may justly have been proud for, as a result, not only was their country actually free again for a time, but they felt themselves to be more than ever one people in their own country.

Bruce was now firmly on the throne, duly endorsed when the bishops and nobles issued the Declaration of Arbroath in 1320, calling upon the Pope to recognise Scotland as an independent kingdom with King Robert as their king.

Bruce is recorded as having had dealings with another

MacFarlane when, as Robert I, he granted a charter of lands of Kindowie and Argushouche to a Dougal MacFarlane, but it is not known who this Dougal was. Perhaps he was at Bannockburn.

Robert I died in 1329 and was succeeded by his son, David II (1329–1337). David was only five years old when he succeeded, and for the next twelve years there had to be Guardians for Scotland. Randolph, Earl of Moray, had been appointed by David's father but after a year Edward Balliol, supported by barons who had been disciplined by Bruce by confiscation of their lands, thought he would try to regain the crown. Randolph died just as he was about to do battle with Balliol; when his successor, Donald, Earl of Mar, was defeated at Dupplin Moor in 1332, Balliol then had himself crowned King.

Within months the new King was himself surprised by his enemies and took refuge in England. The next year, supported by Edward III, he inflicted a shattering defeat upon Sir Archibald Douglas, the then Guardian of Scotland, at the Battle of Halidon Hill. This was the worst defeat the English had ever inflicted upon the Scots. The latter were so badly led that they left their strong hillside position to cross over marshy ground to attack the English who held an advantageous position on the opposite hill. Moreover, the Scots did this not as a piece of military strategy, but solely because they were verbally incited by the enemy.

It was a grievous blow for Scotland. The Guardian himself was killed together with six earls, seventy barons, five hundred knights and squires and a vast number of spearmen. Among the casualties was Malcolm, 5th Earl of Lennox. No one knows how many MacFarlanes fell beside him. The young King David was sent to France for greater protection, and the Guardian representing him, Sir Andrew Moray, continued to attack the English whenever possible, but in effect Balliol and Edward shared Scotland between them.

VI
Getting a Name

In 1329, Malduin's son, Parlan, became fourth Chief of the Clan. We have seen that most historians regard Gilchrist as the first Chief because he was the first to receive the charter for the traditional clan lands centred on Arrochar. Others regard this fourth Chief as the first, because it is from him that the Clan takes its name. Certainly Parlan's grandfather was known as Duncan MacGilchrist, and his father as Malduin, son of Gilchrist (i.e. MacGilchrist), and he himself, perhaps as a child, was known as Parlan MacGilchrist. It is not known why his descendants should have adopted his name as the Clan surname.

It is known that among many clans, as the sons moved away from the home estate, some of them took a different surname. This may have been done for clearer identification or, in some cases, to escape those who sought them for some breach of the law. No doubt some were also identified by their occupations. In the case of the MacFarlanes, some of those who settled in Kirkton, Markinch and Balengowan were descendants of an Allen MacFarlane, and called themselves Allen. Other Chiefs' sons were called Thomas and Walter, whose families became known as Thomson and MacWalter. A study of the Septs of Clan MacFarlane shows that there was a MacNiter (i.e. son of the Weaver) and even Weaver by itself. Those who retained the original surname of MacFarlane in accordance with the wide-spread custom of the time, spelt it in a variety of ways which persist to this day. At one stage the name in the family coat of arms appears as MacPharlan.

We would like to know why the Clan took its name from this fourth Chief. So little is known about him, yet there must have been something outstanding about him for the change to have occurred. When we look at contemporary history there is nothing we can suggest with confidence.

Parlan received his charter from Donald, 6th Earl of Lennox, in about 1344 and, as we have seen, he lived at a period of Scotland's history that can with justice be described as unhappy. The English eventually became so embroiled in what was to become the Hundred Years War with France that they withdrew from Scotland. Balliol could not sustain his struggle without their assistance so the young King David was able to return to Scotland from France after an absence of seven years. Now aged seventeen, he assumed power for himself and led a force against the English at Neville's Cross, near Durham, where he was defeated and taken prisoner. After eleven years he was released on an agreement to pay a huge ransom of £160,000 over ten years. In fact only two instalments were paid but, considering the fact that he led a life of selfish luxury, neither he nor the raising of the ransom gave any pleasure to the Scots people.

Where did Parlan stand in all these matters? Had he taken his place beside the King at Dupplin Moor? Had he, unlike the King, managed to escape among Robert the Stewart's forces after the battle? We do not know.

At any rate, from now on the name of the Clan is MacFarlane.

VII

An Honourable Decision

Parlan was succeeded by his son, Malcolm, who was now the fifth Chief of the Clan. In about 1344 he was confirmed in his lands by a charter granted by his cousin Donald who, on the death of his father, had become the sixth Earl of Lennox. The witnesses to this charter were 'Malcolm Fleming of Wigton, John Stewart of Darnley and Patrick Fleming of Weddal (soldiers)'. Ten years later he received another charter signed at Balloch on May 4th, 1354, in which he and his heirs were discharged of the four mark feu duty payable annually out of the lands.

On the death of King David, his cousin, Robert II (1371–1390) succeeded. Robert was the seventh member of his family to hold the office of steward, which led to him and his family being known as Stewarts, he himself being the first in the Stewart royal line. Robert was a peaceable man, but this did not free him from the necessity of getting involved in his country's troubles. These were mainly lawlessness at home, the barons and the clans in continual contention with each other, and harassment from the English. So weak was the King in such matters that he left the defence of the country to the nobles; indeed, in 1390 he was regarded as so useless that his third son, the Earl of Fife, was made Guardian of the country.

The English persisted with their efforts to conquer both France and Scotland, and this led Robert into making a treaty which resulted in the arrival of a large party of Frenchmen well supplied with arms and money. This may have been a militarily prudent move, but the Scots and French quickly

21

learnt that they did not like each other very much, nor each other's way of life nor methods of fighting their enemies.

When Richard II invaded Scotland he found that he was given no opportunity to fight in a pitched battle; so he withdrew, causing as much slaughter and destruction as he could. Under the leadership of the Earl of Fife and the Earl of Douglas, the Scots undertook an invasion of revenge. This was successfully carried out in 1388 at the Battle of Otterburn – or Chevy Chase, as the English called it.

The sixth Earl of Lennox died in 1373 leaving no son to succeed him. Under these circumstances, according to normal feudal practice, he would have been succeeded by Malcolm MacFarlane, who was 'grandson's grandson of Gilchrist fourth son of Earl Alwyn'. But the Earl had taken the unusual step of leaving the whole estate to his daughter, the Countess Margaret, and Malcolm MacFarlane, believing that he did not have sufficient estate to support the role of a Lennox Earl (which he had no intention of seizing from the Countess), made the honourable decision and declined to put forward his claim. Over one hundred years later a MacFarlane Chief was to make the opposite decision and advance what he believed to be his legitimate claim to the Lennox title, with disastrous results for the Clan.

More important matters than this were being faced in the country generally. Robert was succeeded as king by his son, Robert III (1390–1406). He was elderly for the job, peaceable and unfortunately weak. So it came about that his brother, the Earl of Fife, continued to act as Guardian, just as if the King did not exist. Some of the nobles resented this and thought that Robert's son and heir, the Earl of Carrick, ought to be made Guardian. When this happened in 1399, he showed himself quite unsuitable for the task, with the result that, with the King's consent, the guardianship reverted to the Earl of Fife, who by this time had been made Duke of Albany. Naturally the Earl of Carrick, by now made Duke of Rothesay, was very aggrieved and a bitter enmity developed between the two dukes. In the course of their rivalry, Rothesay was imprisoned by Albany and later died, or was killed in prison.

The King's other son, James, being only twelve years old, was sent to France for protection but on the way was captured by English pirates. On being sent to Henry IV he was put in prison and there he remained for eighteen years. The news of his imprisonment so distressed his father that a few days later, on April 4th 1406, he died. As we shall see, James' bitterness over his imprisonment and his conviction that Albany and others had failed in their duty to secure his release, was to have dire repercussions on the House of Lennox with which the MacFarlanes had such close ties of loyalty and relationship.

VIII

Under a Weak King

At the Mansion House, Inchmirin, on June 10th 1395 Duncan, the sixth Chief of Clan MacFarlane, received the charter confirming his lands from Duncan, 8th Earl of Lennox. This charter describes the territory slightly differently from the one already quoted, referring to the lands

> between the river Dynach and Aldanchwhyn on the one side, and the rivers Arnan, Innis and Trostane on the other side, with the Islands of Elanvow, Elanvanow, Elandowglas and Elaig, in the Earldom of Lennox.

The witnesses to this charter are Walter Buchanan of that Ilk, Humphrey Colquhoun the Laird of Luss, Neil of Balnory, Duncan Campbell of Gaunan and Malcolm McAlpine. The same year, Duncan's wife Christine, a daughter of Sir Colin Campbell of Lochow (an ancestor of the Dukes of Argyll), received a charter for more lands designated as Keanlochlong, Inveriock, Glenluin and Portcable.

Duncan and Christine had two sons – John who succeeded his father as Chief, and Thomas, the founder of the Clachbuy family, some of whom went to the Western Isles and later called themselves Thomson and MacCause. Duncan was Chief in the reign of Robert III, whom we have already seen to have been a singularly weak king, and also in the period when the King's brother, the Duke of Albany, served as Regent in the first place because of the King's weakness and, secondly, during the imprisonment of the young James I. The result of this weakness in the monarchy tempted the English to think that the country was available for the taking. Indeed,

24

Henry personally led an army to besiege Edinburgh Castle.

Within the country there was a further breaking down of law and order, and the inevitable jockeying for power among the nobles with the great Douglas family emerging as the chief threat to the crown. The King's brother, Alexander, became such a wild and vicious outlaw that he was known as 'the Wolf of Badenoch'. In the Highlands, clan members passed their time in descending upon their Lowland neighbours to steal cattle and crops. It was a time when the power of life and death lay in the hands of the chiefs who could make use of the sword and gallows with little restraint. There is a hill at Tarbet where some, justly or unjustly, must have met their end. It is called 'The Gallow Hill', or Tom na Croich.

A remarkable instance of what could happen when the law was held in such disrespect took place when thirty members from each of the clans, Chattan and Kay, settled an inter-clan difference by fighting in an almost gladiatorial battle with an audience of thousands looking on, including the King himself. Of the sixty men involved, forty-nine were killed and the surviving eleven all wounded.

It should be noted at this point that the religous development of Scotland was also changing. People were beginning to ask questions about the truth or otherwise of the teachings of the Roman Catholic Church. A Lollard, James Risby, was burned at the stake in Perth in 1407 for preaching against the doctrines of Rome. Religious issues would stir and then inflame Scotland's life for many years to come.

IX
A Low Profile

When John MacFarlane became the seventh Chief of the Clan, the charter confirming his lands was given under the great seal of James I in 1430. At this date the King was still in exile in England, so the charter must have been confirmed by the regent Albany. The Chief lived under two kings – James I (1406–1437) and, for four years, James II (1437–1460)

In 1420 Duncan, 8th Earl of Lennox, persuaded the General Council to accept his son in-law Murdoch as Regent. Murdoch had been in prison with his king, James I, so it must have been a bitter pill for the King when Murdoch was released in exchange for the Earl of Northumberland. When the King himself was released in 1424, he returned from his exile burning with a sense that he had been neglected and might have been released much earlier if those in power had so wished. He revealed himself as a vindictive man. There were scores to be settled. There was a ransom of £40,000 to be raised in six years. There were wild nobles and chiefs to be brought to heel, and law and order to be enforced. He determined to show who was master in his land.

The King began by decreeing laws that, if enforced, would without question establish much needed order in the country. He then turned to the House of Lennox. First, he imprisoned the eighth Earl and his son-in-law Murdoch, the Duke of Albany, husband of Countess Isabel, as well as their two sons Walter and Alexander. This imprisonment of the Lennox family proved too much for the third son, the illegitimate James, who registered his anger by attacking and setting fire to Dumbarton with the loss of some lives. This James, for the understandable reason of self-preservation, called himself Sir Aulay Macaulay. Although it is not known exactly what charge was laid against the Lennox family, this act at Dumbarton spurred on the King's desire for vengeance, resulting in the execution of his prisoners on Heading Hill at Stirling Castle in 1425. These executions were fully in line with the King's policy at this time. He showed himself equally ruthless towards his own Stewart family when he deprived them of both their property and their dukedoms.

Filled with contempt for the Highland clans he summoned the chiefs to Inverness. Fifty of them came and he arbitrarily hanged some and imprisoned others. His treatment of some clans has been described as little more than outright robbery. The King's actions resulted in, firstly, the restoration of some kind of law and order and, secondly, a vast improvement in his own finances through the confiscations.

Little is known about the doings of MacFarlane's seventh Chief. His name appears on a charter dated 1426, but it is highly probable that as he observed all that was going on he thought it wise to maintain as low a profile as possible since his feudal loyalty lay with the Lennox family, and the King's displeasure might easily turn in his direction. It could not have been easy for him to have lived in quiet obscurity since he was married to Jean, a daughter of Sir Adam Mure of Rowallan, whose other daughter, Elizabeth, was the first wife of King Robert II.

In the course of his policy of breaking the power of the barons, the King made a bitter enemy of Sir Robert Graham. Sir Robert carried his hostility to the lengths of planning revenge and eventually killing the King in a monastery in Perth at Christmas-time in 1436. In those days people did not easily forget or forgive, and the Queen, a daughter of the Earl of Somerset, did not rest until Graham had been caught, cruelly tortured and then executed.

The MacFarlane Chief had witnessed the King's strenuous efforts to subdue the powerful in the land, and he was to see a renewal of the struggle for power among the great barons during the reign of James II (1437–1460), the new King who was only six years old when his father was murdered. The contest chiefly involved three great families: the Crichtons of whom William was the Governor of Edinburgh Castle; the Livingstone family, with Alexander, the Governor of Stirling Castle; and the Douglas family, with Alexander, the fifth Earl of Douglas, as Regent. There was much chopping and changing of loyalties as moves for power were made, causing a great deal of unrest.

When the King was nineteen he married Mary of Gueldres in Holland, and from then on began to exert his authority. With imprisonment and executions he first reduced the Livingstones, then the Crichtons, and finally the most powerful of them all, the Douglas family. From the ruthless ways in which he achieved his purpose the nobles knew that they had met their match.

Such were the life and times of Clan MacFarlane's seventh Chief.

X

The Clan Spreads Out

On his father's death Duncan inherited the chieftainship, the eighth, on January 18th 1441, which he was to exercise for forty-seven years. At this time, the Countess Isabel, the daughter of the eighth Earl of Lennox, would have been a sad woman for some sixteen years, mourning the execution of her father, her husband and two of her sons at the hands of the vindictive king. The Chief of Clan MacFarlane would therefore have had no great feudal lord from whom the Clan could have found support, and to whom they would have given their loyalty.

In 1460, having ruthlessly restrained some of the more rebellious nobles, James II decided to try to regain Berwick-on-Tweed and Castle Roxburgh from the English. The moment seemed opportune as the English were involved in the Wars of the Roses. The castle was eventually taken but not until after the death of the King, for he was killed when a cannon he was standing beside exploded during the attack. This meant that once again there had to be a regent, or guardian, appointed, since the King's son was only eight years of age at his father's death. Bishop Kennedy, the King's cousin was appointed. The unsettled state of affairs that resulted was due to the fact that James II had made many enemies in the process of reducing the power of the nobles. Also, the new Regent, in exercising his authority, supported the Lancastrians thus making enemies of the Yorkists. When the Yorkist Edward IV came to the throne he therefore had scores to settle with the Scots, and there were disgruntled nobles such as the Earls of Douglas and Ross who were very ready to help him.

James III in due course married Princess Margaret of Denmark and assumed power for himself. He proceeded to alienate the nobles further by having as friends and advisers favourites, men who were greatly despised and whose advice was as feeble as they were weak. So incensed were the nobles that some of these favourites were captured and hanged over Lauder Bridge.

Of more immediate interest to us is the fact that the eighth MacFarlane Chief had two sons. Whom he had married we do not know. The elder son, Walter, succeeded him; John, the younger son, was the ancestor of the MacFarlanes of Kenmore on Lochlomondside, from whom are descended the MacFarlanes of Muckroy in Argyllshire, the MacFarlanes of Auchinvenal More in Glen Fruin, and the MacFarlanes of Dunnamaninch in Northern Ireland.

Here again we see members of the Clan moving away from the home estate at Arrochar. It is possible that it was some of these in Muckroy, rather than members of the Chief's own family, who were involved in the Battle of Stalc. This battle was yet another example of inter-clan fighting, and took place in 1468 in Appin, Argyllshire. On one side were the Stewarts and MacLarens, and on the other the MacDougalls and the MacFarlanes. On this occasion the MacFarlanes were on the losing side, for the former clans were successful in defending Dugald, the Chief of Appin, who was a son of John Stewart, the Lord of Lorn and Innermeath. It is reported that some hundreds of men lost their lives.

A stone commemorating this battle was erected at the site by Lt. Col. A. King Stewart of Acknacor in Appin. There are ruins of Castle Stalker still on an island in Loch Laich. The Stewarts had built this castle and ruled the territory all round over many centuries, but no doubt they had to struggle to maintain their position of power from time to time.

XI
On the King's Side

In 1486, towards the end of the reign of James III, Duncan's son, Walter, became the ninth Chief. He is specifically mentioned in a charter given by the King to the town of Dumbarton. Walter married Gertrude, a daughter of James, 2nd Lord Livingstone. She gave him two sons – the elder, Andrew, who succeeded him as Chief, and Dugald, through whom the MacFarlanes spread out still further when he founded the family in Tullichintaul around Glen Douglas, and from whom come the MacFarlanes of Finart and Gorton.

If we look back to the death of Donald, 6th Earl of Lennox, in 1373, we remember that, having no son, he bequeathed his whole estate to his daughter Margaret who married Walter de Fassalane. According to feudal practice the Earl's cousin, Malcolm MacFarlane, had the strongest claim to the Lennox earldom, but believing that he did not possess a large enough estate to support that high office he declined the title. It therefore passed to Walter de Fassalane, whose wife, however, did not let him use the title and so he was known as the Lord of the Lennox.

It was Walter and Margaret's son, Duncan, the eighth Earl of Lennox who was executed by James II, together with his son-in-law and two of his grandsons. When his daughter, Countess Isabel, also died claims were made for the vacant title by Walter MacFarlane, the ninth Chief, as well as by descendants of the Countess' two sisters. One claimant was Sir John Haldane, a descendant of the sister, Margaret, who had married Sir Robert Monteith. The other claimant was descended from the other sister, Elizabeth, who had married a John Stewart of Darnley.

Some believe that Walter MacFarlane's claim was legally the strongest, but on his putting it forward there followed yet another example of a struggle for power of which Scottish history provides so many sad and vicious instances. In 1452, Darnley simply assumed the title and proceeded to make forays from strongholds at Inchmirin and Catter in Lennox territory into MacFarlane lands around Arrochar. The powerful Darnley house brought the MacFarlanes to almost total ruin; the Chief and all his family perished and the only clan members to survive were those who took refuge in remote places. At any rate, Darnley overcame all opposition and in 1473 obtained a Royal Precept declaring him to be the heir to half the lands and to the title, 'Earl of Lennox'.

It is suggested that Clan MacFarlane survived only because of 'help given by a gentleman of the Clan in some matter to the Darnley family'. It has also been put forward that this 'gentleman' had no claim to the chieftainship other than the fact that he was of sufficient power to have been of help to a powerful family, and of sufficient status to have later married Darnley's daughter. Certainly this was the time when the MacFarlanes' centuries old link with the Lennox family was broken, for, in addition to personal antagonism, they were also on opposite sides in national affairs, Darnley being with the barons and MacFarlane with the King.

James III was foolish enough not to learn from the savage event at Lauder Bridge in 1482, for he replaced his inept favourites by others equally unpopular. The nobles decided to replace the King with his son, James IV. There followed the usual taking of sides – those for the King confronting those for his son. The issue was settled at the Battle of Sauchieburn in 1488 when the King's army was destroyed. The King himself, injured when thrown from his horse, took refuge in a cottage where he was stabbed as he lay helpless. Walter MacFarlane, ninth Chief, fell at Sauchieburn fighting for his king – a king whose faults were obvious, but whose good points are usually glossed over by the historians. He was a man – however weak and foolish – of great cultural interests in architecture, painting, literature, poetry, music and calligraphy. If he did not heap honours and gifts upon those who felt entitled to them at least he took on his enemies face to face, and the MacFarlanes were ready to stand with him.

There is a story relating to what is supposed to have happened after the death of Walter, recorded by a one-time minister at Arrochar, the Rev. James Dewar. It is difficult to fit the story neatly into an historical context, but this is how it is told:

In the reign of James III of Scotland, the Laird of MacFarlane was slain at the Battle of Sauchie-burn, near Stirling, in the year 1488, leaving a widow, who was an Englishwoman, the mother of one son; he also left a son by his first wife, who was the heir; but this son and heir had the misfortune to be proud, vain, silly, and a little weak-minded. His half-brother was possessed of a beautiful piebald horse, which had been given to him by some of his mother's relations. The elder brother was about to set out for Stirling and was very desirous of riding this horse, wishing, as the young chief, to make a very grand appearance.

The step-mother refused the loan of the animal, alleging, as her reason for so doing, her fear that it would not be safely brought back. Her denial only made the young man the more persistent. Finally, a written agreement was drawn up, and signed by the heir, in which he promised to forfeit to his half-brother his lands of Arrochar, in case the horse was not safely returned.

The step-mother bribed the groom in attendance to poison the horse on the second day from home, and the estate accordingly went to the younger brother.

Another account states that 'the step-mother caused the stuffing of the saddle to be saturated with poison, which being absorbed by the horse, proved fatal to it.'

The Clan, however, would not acknowledge the younger brother as Chief, but remained loyal to the now landless first son. Some years later the lands were restored to the heir by a special Act of Parliament. The interesting thing about this strange story is that it appears that in the Lennox family there were some MacFarlanes referred to as the 'followers of the piebald horse' and others known as 'followers of the heir'. The Rev. Dewar notes that some have claimed the home of the dispossessed heir to be marked by the ruins of a gable-end on Tullich Hill, above Arrochar.

XII
Ruin, Restoration, Disaster

The battle of Sauchieburn (1488) deprived Andrew, the tenth Chief, of both his king, James III, and his father, Walter. This may well have been the moment when he thought it right to make his peace with John Stewart, the new Earl of Lennox. We have seen how it is believed that this came about, and there is reason for suggesting that the 'gentleman of the Clan' was none other than the new Chief. The breach must certainly have been mended when Andrew married Barbara, the Earl's daughter. So it appears that through Andrew peace was restored between the families resulting in a complete change from a course of total ruin to the restoration of the Clan's fortunes. The Chief now gave his loyalty to the new line of Lennox Earls as fully as his forbears had to the old line.

On the wider Scottish scene changes were also taking place as the old feudal system began to alter. James IV came to the throne in 1488 and quickly began to show that he could give a royal lead in many other directions than in military prowess. Education and learning, the enforcement of impartial law and a more efficient basis of finance, added to his own personal attractiveness all tended to make him popular. He was wise in the way he went about bringing some of the nobles to heel, seeking to win them over to him rather than by crushing them ruthlessly. By taking away with one hand he disciplined them, and by giving with the other he made them his friends.

Henry VII in England kept aggravating the relationship between the countries with warlike incursions, and James

35

retaliated by supporting Perkin Warbeck's efforts to win the English crown. Relations improved when Warbeck had been removed and James had married Henry's daughter, Margaret Tudor. This more peaceful situation lasted until Henry's death, but when Henry VIII came to the throne he tried to adopt bullying tactics and the old enmity returned. On Henry's going to war with France, against his nobles' advice, James stood by 'The Auld Alliance', and this led to the Scots and the English meeting on the fateful Flodden Field.

Some time after 1494 Andrew MacFarlane was succeeded as Chief by his son, John. This new Chief (the eleventh) married a daughter of James, 1st Lord Hamilton, and a niece of James III. Lord Hamilton's other daughter, Elizabeth, was married to Matthew, 2nd Earl of Lennox. This meant that the Chief was related to both the Crown and the Lennox Earl. John MacFarlane was in fact married three times. By his first marriage he had two sons – Andrew, his heir; and Robert, who founded the family at Inversnaid. His second marriage was to a daughter of Herbert, Lord Herries. She gave him a son, Walter, later of Ardleish, the founder of the MacFarlane families of Gartartan and Ballaggan. It is possible that she had another son, Malcolm Beg MacFarlane. John's third wife was Lady Helen Stewart, a daughter of the third Earl of Athole, and she had a son and a daughter, John and Grizel. Which of his wives was the mother of another son, Duncan, is not known but he is mentioned in two documents – the first was a feudal service bond dated 1545, the other was a complaint lodged by the Colquhouns against four named MacFarlanes, of whom he was one.

At some time John MacFarlane was knighted by James IV. In a charter given to a William MacFarlane concerning lands of Garrowstuck, the Chief of the Clan is designated 'the Honourable Sir John MacFarlane, lord of the same, soldier, captain of Clan MacFarlane, son of Andrew, etc.' From this it would appear that his knighthood was bestowed for military ability. The honour was clearly not misplaced for, like his grandfather at Sauchieburn, he lost his life fighting for his king in 1514 at the Battle of Flodden. He was 'one of the flowers of the forest.' This disastrous battle for the Scots resulted in ten thousand men losing their lives on the Scottish side. Among the fallen were the King, thirteen earls, two abbots, as many lords, an archbishop, a bishop, three Highland chiefs, and many others including Matthew, Earl of Lennox, and John, eleventh Chief of Clan MacFarlane. The victory was not exploited by the English, so independence continued; yet 'for many a day afterwards, Scotsmen had to mourn the fatal fight at Flodden, but they remembered it also with pride, as in no field had the Scots shown greater courage.'

XIII
Lawless Times

After Flodden, Andrew MacFarlane succeeded his father to become the twelfth Chief. He was to know sixteen years of a regency before James V (1513–1542) took the reins of power for himself. Most of the great families had lost someone at Flodden, and the House of MacFarlane was no exception. It meant that there was a renewal of inter-family strife as the nobles made their bids for positions of power. This struggle became polarised between the Douglas family led by the Earl of Angus and the Hamiltons led by the Earl of Arran.

Although the old king, James IV, had appointed Queen Margaret as Regent there were those who wanted Albany in her place, as well as those who supported other great families. Eventually, and not very successfully, Albany did rule, but was forced to withdraw to France. The Douglas family then triumphed over the Hamiltons, and for a while held the young king in their hands. They treated him in such a way as to make an enemy of him, as they were to learn to their cost when in 1528 he managed to escape to Stirling Castle and there assumed power of government for himself. The new King, James V, then set about bringing the nobles under his authority. This he did by being completely ruthless towards them. However vindictive he may have felt towards them (and he had good reason), he saw them as lawless beyond all tolerance, and he resolved to establish law and order once more in his kingdom.

At the time of the regency central government had so much on its hands that the remoter areas such as the Highlands had reverted to their old ways. There is abundant evidence of lawlessness and members of Clan MacFarlane were both victims and perpetrators of it. It is recorded in the Privy Seal Register for January 30th 1527 that the Buchanans had made a raid upon the MacFarlanes. It refers to

> treasonable art, part, and assistance, given by them [various members of the Buchanan family and their accomplices], for the treasonable raising of fire in the lands of Arrochar, pertaining to MacFarlane; and for the cruel slaughter of John Laurenceson and certain others, being with him in his company, and for the reiff, spoiling and harrying of the said town of Fowghe, that same time for XIX years.

It will be remembered that Haldane of Gleneagles was one of those who, by reason of his marriage, put in a claim to the Lennox title. Haldane had died at Flodden and a certain Squire Meldrum set out to win the hand of his widow at Strathearn. Meanwhile the MacFarlanes attacked Boturick Castle on the south-east shore of Loch Lomond, this being Haldane's property. They may well have done this out of loyalty to the new Earl of Lennox, but that it was unlawful there can be no doubt.

Another reference to inter-clan strife involving the MacFarlanes appears in Pitcairn's Criminal Trials dated August 16th 1536, in which we read that the new Chief's step-brother, Walter MacFarlane, had to find cautioners for his appearance in court at Dumbarton to face a charge

> for art and part of convocation of the lieges in great numbers, in warlike manner, and besetting the way of Margaret Cunningham, widow of the late Sir John Colquhoun of Luss, and David Farneley of Colmistoune, being for the time being in her company, for their slaughter and for other crimes.

Since Margaret Cunningham married again after this date, some part of these charges cannot have been true.

James V acted to stamp out all such acts of lawlessness and it is possible that since Andrew MacFarlane spent a good deal of time at court he was aware of just how determined the King was in these matters. Nevertheless yet another example of lawless activity is seen in the very year Andrew died (1544), when he and his two brothers – Robert of the Inversnaid family, and Duncan – were all named in a complaint made by John Colquhoun of Luss, regarding a very substantial raid allegedly made by over six hundred men in robbing both property and animals from the Luss estate.

The twelfth chief married a Lady Margaret Cunningham. The authorities are not clear as to who was her father. Some say it was William, Earl of Glencairn, the Lord High Treasurer of Scotland; others, that he was Cuthbert, 3rd Earl of Glencairn. At any rate, they had two sons – Duncan (who was the heir), and George of Markinch, from whom was descended the Ballancleroch branch of the family in Kirkton, Campsie, Stirlingshire. Sir Walter Scott was a friend of a John MacFarlane of this family, even if the rest of the Clan did not fare too well at his hands.

Andrew seems to have been an interesting man. It is believed that he composed the clan pibroch, 'Thogail nam Bò', the name of the Clan's gathering tune. The words accompanying this tune provide an insight as to how at least some MacFarlanes spent their time – helping themselves to their neighbours' cattle! It was an occupation in which many, perhaps most, of the Highland Chiefs of the time indulged.

> We are bound to drive the bullocks,
> All by hollows, hirsts, and hillocks,
> Through sleet and through rain,
> When the moon is beaming low,
> On frozen lake and hills of snow,
> Bold and heartily we go,
> And all for little gain.

The reference to the moon reminds us that in some areas the moon was known as 'MacFarlane's Lantern', since it was by its light that they made their raids. Perhaps it was while they were so engaged that they earned the description of them given by Walter Scott in his poem, 'Cadzow Castle' – 'Wild MacFarlane's plaided Clan'. Although the origin of it is not known, there is another pipe tune associated with the Clan, namely, the march – 'Spaidsearachd Chlann Pharlain.' Efforts to trace this tune have so far proved unsuccessful. Many tunes are known by several names so it certainly exists somewhere.

Andrew MacFarlane possessed another unusual ability which perhaps he learned while travelling abroad – tricks of sleight of hand. He is known to have been in Rome in the company of Alastair MacDonnell, one of the chiefs of Keppoch. Andrew's skill was well enough known to earn him the title 'The Wizard of Luss'. Not unnaturally for the time, there were those who attributed his skill to witchcraft, and it may have been this explanation which gave rise to a story recorded in MacLeod's History of Dumbarton. The story tells of how 'the Wizard' was returning from Linlithgow and, arriving at Patrick Mill near Helensburgh, asked for a drink of water for himself and his horse. The miller refused this simple request, and to punish him Andrew is alleged to have cast a spell over the women workers and the work came to a halt. The women started to dance around crying out, 'Up with the dance! MacFarlane sought a drink and did not get it!' Eventually, the miller asked for the removal of the spell, and everything went on normally!

XIV
A Patriot

Whatever their station in life, James V was quite ruthless towards those who broke the law. Some, particularly among the humbler folk, thought of him as a good king, but he continued to have trouble with the nobles, and even more trouble from the ambitions of Henry VIII. In addition to social and political difficulties, James was ruling at a time when religious issues were also causing further divisions in the country. Henry was determined to break the Scots link with France, and sent an army which led to the battle in the marshes of Solway Firth. The constant quarrelling between the Scots leaders was eventually to result in their complete ruin.

When James V died in 1542 he was succeeded by his daughter, Mary, Queen of Scots. Mary was only one week old at the time and there followed the inevitable string of regents who had to deal with the immense matter of the Protestant Reformation, and also the question of the direction of future political allegiance – with France or with England.

Against this background Duncan, the thirteenth Chief of Clan MacFarlane, succeeded his father in 1544, and living at this period it was almost inevitable that he would have to be a fighting man. Throughout the land Scotsmen were dividing. Some were ready to fight for their Catholic faith, some were equally ready to die for the Reformed faith. Some wished to stand by the Auld Alliance with France, others saw a more peaceful future with England, and many were grimly determined to fight for the freedom of the Scottish people against all comers.

The first regent was James, second Earl of Arran, who, although most Scots disagreed with him, managed, with the return of prisoners from the Battle of Solway Firth, to agree to Henry's plan that the young Queen Mary should marry his son Edward when she reached the age of eleven. However, the pro-France and pro-Catholic party led by the Queen's mother, Mary of Lorraine, and Cardinal Beaton with most of the nobles on their side, got possession of the young Queen, and the marriage contract was broken. At the same time they initiated a persecution of the Protestants.

This repudiation of the marriage led Henry to send a series of invading armies to Scotland, causing terrible suffering and destruction, for which Cardinal Beaton was blamed. For this and for his treatment of the Protestants the Cardinal was eventually murdered. The Regent Arran and the Queen Mother made determined efforts to seek the murderers and to punish them. Henry, however, was very persistent and, although he died in 1547, the prepared army invaded Scotland under the leadership of the Duke of Somerset. Even the pro-English party joined Arran to repulse the invaders. The ensuing Battle of Pinkie, 1547, ended victoriously for the English, but at the end of the day another MacFarlane Chief had died for his country.

Duncan, the Chief, had already shown himself not averse to fighting. In 1544 Lennox, the father of Henry Darnley who married Mary, Queen of Scots, took up arms to oppose the Catholic party under the Regent Arran, and Duncan together with three hundred of his men supported him. However, when they met in the Battle of Glasgow Muir, they were defeated and Duncan suffered the penalty of forfeiture. This penalty was later rescinded on the provision of caution amounting to £1000. The sum was raised in only two days, being backed by his friends, Sir John Campbell of Lundy, Sir John Campbell of Calder, John Campbell of Farquhar, Colin Campbell of Ardkynglass, James Campbell of Lawaries, Archibald Campbell of Glen Lyon and Arthur Campbell of

Ardgarthnay. Lennox himself withdrew to England where he married a niece of Henry VIII, Lady Margaret Douglas, who was the daughter of the widow of James I and the Earl of Angus.

In England, Henry supplied Lennox with an army with which he returned to Scotland. At first, they met with some success. Because of his recent forfeiture, Duncan did not openly support Lennox, but he did send one hundred and forty armed men, described as 'well armed in shirts of mail and two-handed swords, which ... did much available service in ... the mountayne countries.' These were led by his uncle Walter MacFarlane of Ardleish. They took the islands of Bute and Arran, defeated the Earl of Argyll, and burned down the castles of Rothesay and Dunoon. However, when they attempted to take Dumbarton Castle, Lennox and Glencairn were defeated. Walter could believe himself fortunate to have received an indulgence, but he also had to find caution for £3000. This was not difficult, and it was found in the persons of Andrew, Lord Evandale, Henry, Lord Methven and Sir John Hamilton of Finnart.

It was inevitable that Duncan should involve himself with Lennox for he was a convinced supporter of Reformation teachings and, indeed, was described by Buchanan of Auchmar, writing in the late sixteenth century, as 'the first man of any importance in Scotland to make an open profession of the Christian (reformed) religion.' Warring against his Catholic neighbours would have seemed to him both right and proper. It was no wonder that he and many others felt as they did. At that time, there were, obviously, godly people whose loyalties tied them to Rome, but the generality of Roman Catholic leaders in Scotland were immoral and ignorant to a degree that is hard to imagine today. One historian writes:

Clerical immorality was one source of scandal in the church, clerical ignorance another. For instance, Bishop Crichton of Dunkeld cheerfully admitted to an apostate priest on trial before him in 1539, that he had never read either the Old or the New Testament, 'and yet,' he said, 'Thou seest I have come on indifferently well.' There was nothing exceptionally scandalous about Crichton's ignorance of the Scriptures; the scandalous thing was that it was perfectly normal.

The habit of warring against neighbours soon resulted in trouble for Duncan. In 1544, the Laird of Luss complained to the government about MacFarlane's activities in despoiling his neighbours generally, and the Colquhouns in particular. Colquhoun's complaint led to the following letter, dated 21st December, going out to the Sheriffs of Argyll, Dumbarton, Renfrew and Stirling, under the seal of Queen Mary, summoning all leiges in these shires to unite with John Colquhoun of Luss in bringing the perpetrators of the named crimes to justice:

That Duncan MacFarlane of Arrochar, Andrew MacFarlane, Robert MacFarlane, and Duncan MacFarlane, his fader, brether,... Ewer Campbell of Strachur, James Stewart, son to Walter Stewart in Balquidder, and certain others, great thieves, limmers [rogues], robbers, common sorners upon our lieges, throatcutters, murderers, slayers of men, women and children,... and their accomplices, to the number of six hundred men, and more, came to the said John's lands and place of Rossdhu, and lands and Barony of Luss, and there cruelly slew and murdered nine of his poor tenants in their beds, and harried his whole country, both himself and his poor men, as well as all in sight, goods within house, as of black cattle, sheep and other beasts, late in the month of December, and daily pursued in plain reiff [plunder] and sorning [obtruding as an unwelcome guest] upon the poor lieges of our realm, and are gathered to them many thieves and limmers intending to harry the whole country to Glasgow and Stirling, if they be not resisted, in high contempt of our authority and law.

The letter provided that if any of the thieves should be killed in the attempt to take them, no crime should attach to the parties killing them, and anyone failing to obey this proclamation would be reckoned to be taking part with the offenders and would be punished accordingly. It is a commentary upon the time, and perhaps also upon the wholesale nature of the accusation, that in spite of the explicit instructions nothing happened. The quarrel with the Colquhouns involved Duncan's uncle Walter, for in 1546 it was alleged against them that 'Robert Dennistoun Colgrain, Walter MacFarlane of Ardleish, Andrew MacFarlane his son, and their accomplices, carried away from Nether and Middle Mains of Luss, sixteen cows to the value of seven merks each.' Sir John Colquhoun did not get any quick recompense, for seven years after the event and three years after the death of Walter others were being summoned to Edinburgh to answer the charge of stealing these cattle.

In 1547 Duncan was involved in more trouble when together with fifty-eight of his followers he attacked the property of Sir Patrick Maxwell and stole 280 cattle, 80 sheep, 24 goats, 20 horses, 80 stones of cheese, 40 bolls of barley and some household furniture. How a matter of such magnitude was settled legally is not clear, but there must have been total forgiveness, for his son and heir was permitted to marry Sir Patrick's daughter, Agnes.

Duncan was married twice; first to Isabel Stewart, a daughter of Andrew, Lord Ochiltree. Isabel died without having any children. Duncan then married Catherine Anne Colquhoun, the fourth daughter of Sir John, the eleventh Chief of Clan Colquhoun and his wife Margaret Stewart, who was a daughter of the first Darnley, Earl of Lennox. Both Catherine's father and her brother who succeeded him had died by the time she married, and her nephew was then the Chief.

There was a further definition of MacFarlane lands made when Duncan and Catherine were invested in liferent in the lands of Arrochar on July 17th 1543, after Duncan's father had surrendered them into the hands of Matthew, Earl of Lennox, for re-investment. The original instrument of Sasine is preserved at Rossdhu and, as quoted by James MacFarlane, reads as follows: 'Jarbolze, Ardlewe, Jarrowstuk, Stukindryne, Ardmurlik, Portcapill, Innerquhilling, Blairrannyth, and Stronfyne, extending annuallly to ten pounds of land of old extent in the Earldom of Lennox and Shire of Dumbarton.'

The witnesses to this document were Robert MacFarlane, Patrick MacFarlane, John MacFarlane Robertson, Donald Macneill, Thomas Macneill, Dowgall Mackcowll, John M'Kynne, Murdoch Makcalpene, and Sir James Lang, Chaplain, and others.

Duncan and his uncle had been in some scenes of violence to which can be attached little glory, but their last fight together saw them fighting for their country. When Duncan lost his life in the Battle of Pinkie, near Musselburgh in September 1547, their army had been badly led, and in its defeat thousands of Scotsmen lost their lives and many were taken prisoner. They fought, although they were Protestants, under the Catholic Arran on the side of the Catholic Queen, but they were men fighting for the independence of their country.

XV

Heroes and Rebels

The next Chief of Clan MacFarlane, the fourteenth, was only three years old when he succeeded his father in 1547. Andrew could not have been aware of what was going on in his country after Pinkie. He would soon learn that his father had died fighting the English; he would learn of all the casualties and the prisoners; of the English consolidating their victory by seizing many strongholds, and hear how, by their subsequent behaviour, they steadily built up an even greater hatred for themselves than had existed before.

The Scots Queen had been sent to France for greater safety and it was not long before the Scots appealed for assistance from the French. Help was soon forthcoming in the form of six thousand trained and armed men who, after some eighteen months of fighting, drove out the English. Unfortunately, by this time, however, the Scots and the French had developed a great and mutual dislike for each other. When the Chief was only ten, Queen Mary of Lorraine, the Queen Mother, had herself made regent and aggravated the anti-French feeling by unwisely putting Frenchmen into many leading and responsible positions. Meanwhile, reformed doctrines won over an ever-increasing number of adherents, with some prominent leaders pledging themselves to make Scotland Protestant. When the Earls of Argyll, Glencairn, Morton and Lord Lorn pledged themselves in this way, the Catholic persecution of lesser people only stirred up bitterness and the awesome oratory of John Knox fanned the flames of trouble. When Andrew MacFarlane was thirteen, the Catholic party, aided by the now hated French, had been

defeated by the Scots helped by English Protestants. The
Scottish Parliament removed the Catholic faith as the
nation's religion, and Reformed Protestant teaching took its
place.

Mary, Queen of Scots, returned from France to her
kingdom when Andrew was seventeen.

As a young man, Andrew MacFarlane appears before us
first as a witness to the resignation by the Rector, Sir
Humphrey Colquhoun, of the rights and fruits of the rectory
of Kilpatrick-Juxta, in favour of Sir James Lang, the chaplain
of the Glasgow diocese. This resignation was made into the
hands of Lord James, Archbishop of Glasgow. Andrew next
appears as a cautioner for Sir John Colquhoun of Luss, for
payments of monies to Humphrey Cunningham, should Sir
John be unable to pay.

The next reference to him is when he shares with John
Colquhoun of Luss, Robert Colquhoun of Camstradden,
William Smollett, burgess of Dumbarton, and Walter
Buchanan of Drumakill the responsibility of a trial
concerning an 'intent to slaughter'. Nine Dumbarton men
all named Houston were found guilty of the charge, and one
other was acquitted. The intended victim was Andrew
Hamilton of Cochno, who had been outlawed after the Battle
of Langside, in which he had fought for Queen Mary. The
whole matter may well have originated in the post-war
animosities which must have permeated Scottish life.

When he was twenty, Andrew married Agnes, a daughter
of Sir Patrick Maxwell of Newark, Port Glasgow. In the
course of time they had three sons and two daughters. The
eldest son, John, succeeded him as Chief. The second son,
George, left no family, though the remains of his old castle
home survive on his former lands in the Mains of
Kilmaronock. The third son was Humphrey of Brackearn.
The elder daughter, whose name is not known, married as
his second wife, Duncan, the seventeenth Chief of Clan
Gregor and had two sons, the second of whom commanded
a division in the Battle of Glen Fruin in 1603. The other

daughter, Elizabeth, married Malcolm MacFarlane of Gartartan. He was of sufficient power and energy to have been indicted, together with his brother-in-law, for the alleged misdeeds of the Clan.

The highlight of his time as Chief must surely have been the visit of his King, James VI, to Andrew's home at his castle on Eilean-a-Vow in Loch Lomond. This castle had been built in 1577 when he was thirty-three, and the King's visit may well have been an acknowledgement of the heroic part Andrew and his men had played at the Battle of Langside. Whatever the King may have thought about the beauty of the locality, he must have considered the meat at table not too palatable, when he remarked, 'MacFarlane's geese like their play rather than their meat.'

Since Langside was an important battle for Scotland we must be clear about its background. After the death of her husband Darnley – for which many of her enemies at the time blamed her, although they themselves were actually responsible – Queen Mary married, with what some thought indecent haste, James, Earl of Bothwell, who was also believed to have played some part in the murder. The nobles refused to have Bothwell as their King and, indeed, Mary herself refused to declare him as such. However, the Queen and the nobles each collected together armies. At Carberry Hill, near Musselburgh, many in Bothwell's army deserted and he fled. He went to Denmark where he was imprisoned and where later, insane, he died.

While he lived, however, Mary would not give up Bothwell, and eventually she was imprisoned by the nobles in Lochleven Castle. After five days she was forced to surrender her throne to her son, James VI, who was only one year old at the time. The old Earl of Moray, a bitter enemy of the Queen and also a Protestant, was appointed regent. After a year, Mary managed to escape and later at Hamilton Palace, surrounded by supporting bishops and barons, she heard them take an oath to restore her to the throne. The Regent collected an army which met Mary's army at Langside, now part of

Glasgow, and the Queen was defeated. She made her escape to England where, after eighteen years of illegal imprisonment, she was executed, being considered a threat to England as a possible focus for Catholic rebellion.

Thus Langside was fought to decide whether Mary or her son James was to rule Scotland. The battle had been a short but tough struggle and some historians record the fact that the MacFarlanes played a decisive role in it. Many nobles supported Mary, but Andrew MacFarlane, who was twenty-four at the time, allied himself with the young King and the Regent. It was perhaps natural that he should have so decided, for not only was he a Protestant, but he also owed allegiance to the House of Lennox and he may well have shared the belief that Darnley, the heir to Lennox, had been killed with the Queen's connivance.

James MacFarlane describes the battle in this way:

> ...at nine o'clock in the morning. The Queen's vanguard charged along the Bus-an-'aik (bush and oak) Road to that part of the field where the Queen's Park Public School is now situated, and up the existing Lang Loan to the village. There they encountered the Regent's spearmen, while his Hagbutters poured a steady fire on the advancing enemy... The Regent's left wing was brought up, and by a flank movement charged the Queen's vanguard... forcing them to turn back after long fighting and pushing and swaying to and fro, as they were locked together in deadly struggle. 'God and the Queen' resounded from one party; 'God and the King' thundered from the other. The fresh attack confused the column of assailants, and the dark, dense, and united line of helmets was broken, and hurled in disorder back upon Clincart Hill....A wild debacle ensued as the now demoralised Queen's troops were swept down the slopes.

The battle did not last as long as an hour, but three hundred men lost their lives in the struggle. Of the crucial role played by the MacFarlanes the historians have no doubt. Hollinshed writes:

> In this battle the valiance of a Highland gentleman named MacFarlane stood the Regent's part in great stead, for in the hottest brunt of the fight he came in with three hundred of his friends and countrymen, and so manfully gave in upon the Queen's people that he was a great cause of disordering them.

Alexander Nisbet writes:

> In defence of which (his religion) he (Andrew) made several signal appearances, particularly at the famous Battle of Langside, fought on May 10th, 1586, at which battle the Earl of Murray, who was then Regent, being almost overpowered by the number of Queen Mary's forces, and his army ready to give way, the Laird of MacFarlane came in very seasonably to his assistance with a considerable supply of three hundred men, with whom he attacked the right wing of the Queen's army so furiously that they were immediately obliged to quit their ground, and betake themselves to their heels, and were soon followed by the rest of the army. He took at the battle three of Queen Mary's standards which were for a long time preserved in the family.
> [It has been claimed that these standards were for a long time preserved in Glasgow Cathedral.]

The verdict of these historians is endorsed by the fact that the Regent acknowledged his indebtedness to the Laird by giving him the crest and motto which are recorded in the Lyon Register, and have been used in the family ever since. The crest depicts a demi-savage proper, holding in his dexter hand a sheaf of arrows, and pointing with his sinister to an imperial crown, with the motto, 'This I'll defend.' The crown is, of course, that of James VI. The grasping of the arrows refers, perhaps, to the mastery of the deadly arrows of the Queen's archers that had been pouring into the Regent's forces.

There is no record of any further rewards being given to Andrew MacFarlane after the battle, but it is reasonable to think of the King's visit to Eilean-a-Vow as having been due in part to the Chief's heroic action in what was a vital battle for the King.

The victory at Langside did not, however, put an end to the struggles for power in Scotland. Mary had appointed the Earl of Arran, the head of the Hamiltons, as her Lieutenant, and a member of his family assassinated the Regent Moray thinking that then the people would rally round Arran. This did not happen. Instead, the Earl of Lennox was appointed in his place. It was a role he filled somewhat ineffectually for only fourteen months, before he too was shot by one of Mary's supporters. For one year there followed the regency of Mar and, after him, for seven years, that of the Earl of Morton. This jostling for position was symptomatic of the insecurity of the times with the country virtually in a state of civil war.

The inevitable result of this state of affairs was a breakdown in law and order, and the Highlands provided ideal territory for the kind of banditry which ensued. It seems that the Chief of MacFarlane, hero though he was at Langside, sat as lightly to laws that did not suit him as did most of his powerful contemporaries. These were days when men felt strongly about their grievances and their causes and, with the enforcement of law being difficult, weak, and often totally absent, each man took his own steps to protect himself and his extended family, the Clan. None were too particular as to the methods they used to secure their protection.

The acts of lawlessness of which the MacFarlanes were (or were alleged to be) guilty, over a period of years led the Clan to the nadir of its fortunes when in 1608 they were declared to be rebels at law. This condemnation did not last long, but the period provided the Clan with a character which the historians have not allowed the world to forget, for which they have not given a full explanation, and which the facts show to have been an unbalanced judgement.

There is, of course, no smoke without fire as we shall see.

On December 2nd 1578 the Earl of Montrose received a commission for the apprehension of the Chief's brother, Duncan, together with Duncan M'Coull MacFarlane and others to face a charge of murder. This commission he fulfilled with the aid of forty supporters, by surrounding, one night, the Mill of Nab, the home of William Drummond. There he violently seized the two Duncans and imprisoned them in Kincardine. Five days later, Patrick, Lord Drummond, complained to the courts about the Earl's action. It was ordered that the captives be produced to stand trial on January 13th. The outcome of the trial is not known, nor are the details of the accusation. There is some confusion over the fact that one reference speaks of two Duncans, whereas another refers to Duncan and his servant Malcolm MacGillevoray.

The name MacFarlane came unfavourably to the King's notice in 1580, for it seems that Malcolm Beg MacFarlane (probably the younger son of Walter of Ardleish) had claimed to be Keeper of the King's Forest of Glenfinlas, and, as we see from the following letter (from the Red Book of Menteith), he is referred to as a contemporary of Andrew MacFarlane:

James, by the Grace of God, King of Scots, to our loved Thomas Wallace, Messenger, Messengers, Sherrifs in that part, 'coniunctlie' and surely, specially constituted, greeting: Forasmuch as it is understood by us and the lords of our Secret Council that, lately, upon the day of November last, bypast, Malcolm Beg MacFarlane, in Letter, upon sinister and wrong information made to us privately obtained our other letter, subscribed with our hand, without the advice of our Council, giving and granting him the custody and keeping of our wood and forest of Glenfinlas, with the deer, therein, for a certain space, as the same at length details; and seeing the same, as we are surely informed, has 'tendit and tendis', altogether to our great hurt and 'lesious', as also

understanding our trusty cousin and councillor Sir
James Stewart of Doune, knight, and his predecessors
are and have been heritably invested in proper form and
heritage in the keeping of the said wood and forest, and
has been in continual possession thereof, to this hour;
and willing that our said trusty cousin and councillor be
in no wise hurt nor deprived in his right and place of the
said wood, but rather fortified and assisted therein, for
his better and surer preservation of the same, our will is
therefore, and we charge you and straitly and command,
that incontinently these our letters shall pass, and in our
name and authority command and charge the said
Malcolm Beg MacFarlane, Andrew MacFarlane of that
Ilk, and all other pretending keepers of our said wood
and forest, to desist and cease from all further
occupation, 'melling', keeping, cutting, or intromitting
with our said wood and forest or any part thereof, within
twenty four hours next after they be charged by you
thereto, under the pain of rebellion and putting of them
to our horn, and if they fail therein, the said twenty four
hours being bypast, that you incontinently thereafter
denounce the disobedience and rebellion, and put them
to our horn and escheet, and inbring all their movable
goods to our use for their contemptiousness; and such
like, that you, in our name and authority pass to the
Market Crosses of our burghs of Stirling, Perth, parish
kirk at Port Kilmadok, and other places needful, and let
there be open proclamation, prohibition, command, and
charge to all and sundry of our lieges and subjects whom
it affects, that they or none of them take upon hand to
do nor attempt anything contrary to the tenour of these
our letters, nor to answer, obey, or acknowledge any
other forester or keeper of our said wood than our said
trusty cousin, heritable fiar, aforesaid, and his deputies,
under all highest pain and charge that after may follow,
certifying them, that if they do anything to the contrary,
they shall be punished therefor with all vigour according

to law and conform to justice, as you will answer to us thereupon; the which to do we commit to you our full power by these our letters, you delivering them duly executed and endorsed again to the bearer, Gavin, under our Signet and subscribed with our hand at Holyrood-House, the vii day of December, and of our reign the xiii year, 1580

James R.

Lennox. C.E. Argyll

In the disturbances that went on – and they were many – the name MacFarlane unfortunately continues to appear. There is an Order dated January 20th 1585, which clearly gives the state of affairs as it appeared to the King and his Council, in the following terms:

The King and his Council being informed that his good and peaceable subjects inhabiting the countries of the Lennox, Menteith, Stirlingshire and Strathearn are heavily oppressed by reif, stouth, sorning, and other crimes, daily and nightly committed upon them by certain thieves, limmers and sorners, lately broken loose upon them from the braes of the country next adjacent, charge is given to a number of lairds, some twenty-eight in number, to attend the Council on the 28th January, under pain of rebellion, to give information as to the repressing of these outrages.

Andrew MacFarlane is on this list of lairds. However, why the Chief did not attend the Council on the required date is not known. Perhaps he remembered what James I had done at Inverness when he so ruthlessly dealt with the chiefs who had offended him. As a result of his non-attendance, an Order from Stirling Castle dated 30th January 1585 ordained that 'as Andrew MacFarlane of the Arrochar, James McCondoquhy MacFarlane in Illinvow, Malcolm Beg MacFarlane in Letter in Stragartney, have not obeyed the summons to appear under pain of horning, it is now ordered that the penalty take effect.'

That the Clan was in trouble there can be no doubt, for the MacFarlane Lairds of Clackon, Dumford, Kirktown and Orquhart are specifically mentioned in Parliamentary Acts of 1585. July 1587 saw no less than nineteen acts passed to try to bring about law and order; and 'for the quieting and keeping in obedience of the disordered subjects, inhabitants of the Borders, Highlands and Isles.' These 'disordered' subjects were described as 'delighting in all mischiefs and most unnaturally and cruelly wasting, slaying, harrying and destroying their own neighbours, and native country people, taking occasion of the least trouble that may arise in the inner parts of the Realm, when they think that care and thought of the repressing of their insolence is in any way relaxed, to renew their most barbarous cruelties and godless oppressions.'

A roll of the names of the landlords and baillies of the lands dwelling on the Borders and in the Highlands 'where broken men have dwelt and presently dwell' contains the Lairds of Buchanan, MacFarlane of the Arrochar, Luss, and MacAulay of Ardincaple, and in a 'Roll of the Clans that have Captains, Chiefs and Chieftains on whom they depend, oftimes against the wills of their landlords, as well on the Borders as in the Highlands, and of some special persons or branches of the said Clans, ordained to be ratified in that Parliament', are the Buchanans, the MacFarlanes of the Arrochar, and the Clan Gregor.

However involved the MacFarlanes really were in all this lawlessness – and the evidence for some involvement is all too clear – undoubtedly there was a reason for it. It might not be too wide of the mark to suggest that the chief reason for their wildness at this period was due to the bitter feud that developed between their clan and that of the Colquhouns. Responsibility for the MacFarlane share of that trouble is often laid more on the shoulders of John, the Chief's son, than on the Chief himself, because in 1581 Andrew resigned his land to Esme, Duke of Lennox, in favour of his son, only retaining to himself a life-rent in the estate. We must look into the reasons for this feud in the proper place but, at the least, it will be seen that the MacFarlanes were not the main nor the only culprits.

Eilean-A-Vow Castle

XVI
A Clan Feud

In the course of their history many clans in Scotland were involved in savage feuds one with another. Clan MacFarlane was no exception. The blame for the fierce and bitter feud between the MacFarlanes and the Colquhouns is placed squarely upon the MacFarlanes by Sir William Fraser – not unnaturally, since he was the historian of Clan Colquhoun. A closer look at the facts makes the actions of the MacFarlanes understandable even if they are not excusable, and reveals that the reasons for them must, however, clearly be laid at the door of the Colquhouns.

The clans were on opposite sides of the religious divide in the civil war so there would have been a natural antipathy between them, and the predatory raids upon each other's property at the time of Duncan, the thirteenth Chief, fell within the normal practice of the time. At the Battle of Langside, when national matters were more important, they found themselves united by their patriotism under the Regent Moray in support of the young King, but this unity was not to last for past grievances were not forgotten.

When Andrew, Duncan's son, was Chief events took on a much more serious aspect. At the heart of the feud there were three factors which are difficult to separate and evaluate in importance. There was the matter of property, the matter of murder, and thirdly a matter of the heart.

Regarding property, we know that on 10th August 1590, nine years after he had handed over his estates to his son John, Andrew MacFarlane was ordered by the courts to pay Sir Humphrey Colquhoun for some specified stolen animals:

40 oxen at £12 each, 60 kye at £8 each, and 10 horses at £13.6s.8d. each. Since these animals appear again in a claim made on January 3rd 1602, clearly they had not been paid for as ordered. Worse still, the raids had continued. Eventually there was an attack on Bannachra Castle during which Sir Humphrey was killed, and the inter-clan feud assumed even more serious proportions.

The nineteenth-century historian Sir William Fraser tells of Sir Humphrey being killed while nobly defending his own and his neighbours' property from the MacFarlanes. Taking refuge in his castle he was killed by a MacFarlane arrow. In this account the crime was compounded by the additional murders of three of his servants, Robert Colquhoun of Tullichintaul, John Galloway, and Gavin MacLellan, together with a brutal assault upon Sir Humphrey's eldest daughter, Jean.

These alleged crimes are recorded in the Privy Council Records, under December 31st 1608, with Dougall MacCoull MacFarlane of Drumfad (but, at that date, of Tullichintaul) being included as one of the culprits. Surety was provided by Parlane MacWalter of Auchenvenal that Dougall would appear to answer the charge at the next travelling court of the Sheriffs of Dumbarton. Justice moved very slowly, for six years later an entry for 13th January 1614 names John, the son of the fourteenth Chief, as included in these crimes. Surety that he would appear for trial was provided by John, Earl of Mar. Another reference to MacFarlane participation in the Bannachra affair is contained in a contract between Alexander Colquhoun and Malcolm MacFarlane of Gartartan, in which Malcolm was released of all the charges against him relating to Bannachra, and to other raids at Colquhoun, Connaltown, and Tullychewan. To have these charges against him dropped and relations restored between his family and the Colquhouns, Malcolm, for his part, had to enter into a bond of man-rent and service to Alexander Colquhoun 'against all men except the Duke of Lennox'. It may seem strange that

the Colquhouns were ready to drop all these charges unless
it was in some way to strengthen their case against the other
MacFarlanes.

The events at Bannachra clearly exacerbated the whole
position between the two clans but, before examining the
story more closely as understood by the Colquhouns, we
must note that they felt they had an enormous claim to make
against the MacFarlanes in terms of property alone, and their
exasperation at the ineffectiveness of the law in dealing with
their claims and the long delay in making any kind of
restitution must have irked them in the extreme. Some idea
of what lay behind their sense of loss can be seen from the
following list of animals allegedly taken by the MacFarlanes
and found preserved at Rossdhu. Such a record alone
explains the animosity roused by this aspect of the feud.

1590	£. s. d.
5 Horses	126. 6. 8.
2 Staiggis	20. 0. 0.
21 Mares and 11 Foals	625. 6. 8.
21 Cows	248. 0. 0.
5 Oxen	62. 0. 0.
20 Sheep	25. 0. 0.
1591	
8 Horses	148. 0. 0.
2 Staiggis	20. 0. 0.
15 Mares and 3 Foals	197. 6. 8.
26 Cows	322.13. 4.
11 Oxen	138. 0. 0.
68 Sheep	102. 0. 0.
1592	
7 Horses	436. 0. 0.
2 Staiggis	26.13. 4.
13 Mares and 5 Foals	262. 0. 0.
34 Cows	357. 0. 0.
10 Oxen	140. 0. 0.

44 Sheep	98. 0. 0.
1593	
1 Horse	20. 0. 0.
1 Stag	10. 0. 0.
3 Mares	36.13. 4.
4 Cows	46. 0. 0.
4 Oxen	56. 0. 0.
8 Sheep	12. 0. 0.
1594	
4 Horses	96.13. 4.
1 Stag	6.13. 4.
20 Mares	197.13. 4.
37 Cows	385. 0. 0.
10 Oxen	132. 0. 0.
24 Sheep	21. 0. 0.
	£4,371. 0. 0.

There is also a statement of the profits lost in these five years by the theft of these animals. James MacFarlane states that the actual sum claimed in full is no less than £155,501.8s.0d. This does not include household furniture, goods and suchlike.

We have recorded something of the Bannachra troubles as seen by the Colquhouns. Not unnaturally, the MacFarlanes saw it all differently. The Rev. James Dewar, at one time the Minister at Arrochar, gives an account which, while not excusing what might have taken place, does explain it rather differently. Dewar's explanation is given credence by an entry in the diary of Robert Birrell, a burgess of Edinburgh, which throws further light upon the murder of Sir Humphrey. Supported as it is by a decree of the Lords in Secret Council dated February 15th 1611, it proves beyond all reasonable doubt that the blame laid on the shoulders of the MacFarlanes should rest elsewhere.

First then, Dewar's account:

In the reign of James VI, MacFarlane's dwelling-house

was at Tarbet, on the shores of Loch Lomond, close to where the school-house now stands. At that time, when the taking of cattle from the Lowlanders was a gentlemanly occupation, MacFarlane levied the 'blackmail' for the rent of the Earl of Lennox's land, and protected the tenants from robbers. He had a band of one hundred men living between Loch Sloy and Tarbet, ready to arm at the shortest notice. He (John, afterwards 15th Chief), was married to a lady by name Buchanan of Kilmaronock. She, as was the custom in that day, spun and made webs of cloth. Her weaver lived at Banairich, a mile below Luss. She often had an excuse to go to his house. There were no roads then, and when she went, it was by boat. Reports of her improper intimacy with Sir Humphrey Colquhoun had reached MacFarlane, and his jealousy was aroused. On one occasion she wished to go to her weaver's with a web. MacFarlane was unwilling to allow her, and desired her to send a servant instead, but she would not listen to his request, and as she was hastily dressing, a note fell from her garments, which her husband lifted, unperceived by her. On reading the paper, he found it contained an arrangement for the meeting, that day, of his lady with Sir Humphrey Colquhoun.

After she had left, MacFarlane aroused his 'Airphi', and marched them down by the most direct road, across Glen Douglas. They crossed Luss Glen at Auchengarna, came through the wood above Banaridhu, and surrounded the house. They could see Mrs MacFarlane and Sir Humphrey walking together. He understood that the MacFarlanes had not come as friends, and fled for refuge to his castle of Bannachra, about five miles distant, and outrunning his pursuers, had all the doors secured before they came up. The MacFarlanes were unable to force the doors, nor did they know in what part of the castle he was concealed, but finding Sir Humphrey's body-servant in an outhouse, they brought him to MacFarlane, who put his sword to the servant's breast, saying, 'Tell me in what part of the castle your master is concealed, or I will run this sword through you.' The poor wretch, thus threatened, told where Sir Humphrey was hidden, when MacFarlane caused his men to bring brush, heather and wood and set fire to them on the windy side of the castle.

The smoke forced Sir Humphrey to open a window for breath, when one of MacFarlane's men shot him with an arrow that gave him a mortal wound. The doors were then opened, and Sir Humphrey was delivered into MacFarlane's hands, who caused him to be beheaded at once, and the body mutilated in revenge.

As they returned they took the gates of the castle of Rossdhu, and set them up at Arrochar where they remained until 1784. The attack on Jean Colquhoun, horrible though it was, at the time would have been regarded in the light of an eye for an eye.

Sir Walter Scott's words in 'The Lady of the Lake' refer to this event:

> Proudly our pibroch has thrilled in Glen Fruin,
> And Bannachra's groans to our slogan replied.

The slogan, of course, refers to the MacFarlane rallying cry, *'Loch Sloy'*; and the pibroch to their gathering tune – *'Thogail nam Bò'*.

That then was the matter of the heart in the feud.

We come now to the diary entry which, as will be seen, clashes with the accounts of Sir Humphrey's death as given by both Fraser and Dewar. Robert Birrell (as researched by Fraser in the nineteenth century), writing in his diary under November 30th 1592, states: 'John Colquhoun was beheaded at the Cross of Edinburgh, for murdering of his own brother, the Laird of Luss.' It has been suggested that, as a servant is known to have been involved in the events of the day at Bannachra, this John Colquhoun of the diary was a servant and not a brother. However, the diary explicitly states 'brother', and it is known that the brother John was in any case an unsavoury sort of person. He had killed a Donald MacNeill MacFarlane, a personal servant of Robert Galbraith of Culcreuch. He had, through this, started a feud between the Galbraiths and the Colquhouns. Certainly it was not John but Alexander who succeeded Sir Humphrey as Chief.

It seems to the writer that the matter is clearly settled not just by the diary entry, but also by the supporting decree of the Lords of Council in excusing Alexander Colquhoun for not producing his tenant and servant John MacDouill Vic Neill MacFarlane, to answer a charge of the murder of a Catherine MacIlerith, on the grounds that to have done so would have revived the feud between the Clan Colquhoun and the Clan MacFarlane. The decree plainly stated that the feud existed 'upon the occasion of the slaughter of Humphrey MacFarlane, father to the said John MacDouill Vic Neill MacFarlane, and was committed by Sir Humphrey Colquhoun of Luss.'

There then is frankly stated, in two sources without any vested interests in the matter, the real reasons for 'that deadly feud and enmity which was of long continuance'.

When exactly the feud was resolved is uncertain, but there were many efforts to bring it to an end. The MacFarlanes always had enough friends to be able to find sureties to come forward at their own financial risk to ensure that they would appear to answer any charge brought against them. Indeed, one of them -William Cunningham – in 1590 had his fingers burnt, for Adam Colquhoun claimed that several of the MacFarlanes had contravened an Order by which he and his family 'should be harmless and skaithless in their bodies, lands, possessions, and goods under various penalties.' He won his claim and MacFarlane's cautioner was ordered to pay the penalties. Clearly, being a surety was no empty gesture.

In 1593, Alexander Colquhoun secured a prohibition preventing Robert Erskine of Sauchie disposing of any of his goods and property, because he had stood surety for Andrew MacFarlane that he would satisfy persons 'scathed' [hurt, injured, damaged]. Alexander clearly thought he would win his case.

In 1597, another attempt was made to heal the breach between the clans, when the Laird of Luss received a bond from the Earl of Mar, John Erskine. It reads as follows:

Be it known to all men by these presents, we John, Earl of Mar, Lord Erskine, for ourself, and taking the burden upon us for Andrew MacFarlane of Arrochar, John MacFarlane his eldest son, fiar thereof, Andrew MacFarlane of Gartartan, Malcolm MacFarlane, his eldest son, fiar thereof, and the remaining surname of MacFarlane, our kin, friends, men, tenants, servants, dependants, assistants, partakers, and all others that are liable to undergo the law, desire to state and, by the tenour hereof, specially and expressly assure Alexander Colquhoun of Luss, his kin, friends, men etc., that they shall be unhurt, unharmed, unmolested, untroubled, uninvaded, or in any wise pursued, criminally or 'eiuilye', in the law, or by the law, by me or our foresaid, for whatsoever cause, quarrel, or occasion bygone, preceding the date hereof, unto the 11th day of November next to come; promising to observe, and cause these presents to be observed and kept inviolate in any point, under the pain of 'periurie', infamy, and loss of perpetual credit, honour, and estimation, in time coming. In witness whereof, we, for our help, and taking the burden upon us, as said, subscribe these presents, as follows, at Stirling Castle, the first day of June, the year of God, fifteen hundred and ninety-seven, before these witnesses, Harry Shaw, Thomas Howme, Charles Panter and Andrew Buchanan, our servants.

J. Mar

A. Buchanan, Witness
Thomas Howme, Witness

On November 7th of the same year, Alexander Colquhoun signed a similar bond which made the truce last until the end of the month.

There is a letter in the Montrose Charter Chest which states in private that the MacFarlanes were ready to satisfy all parties they had injured in the past, except Clan Colquhoun. These noble and placatory sentiments towards others were somewhat modified publicly, when they agreed to make restitution only in cases that were proved against them. It is obvious that there was no desire on either side to heal the breach, despite the efforts of their friends. No redress had as yet been made to the Colquhouns by Andrew, John, Humphrey or Malcolm, so, once more in 1603, the Chief of Colquhoun tried again legally, and obtained a decree from the Lords in Council ordering that redress should be made. Malcolm's friends, particularly those in high places, saw which way the wind was blowing when they urged that the feud should end. The King was getting impatient with the continuing lawlessness in the Highlands and remoter parts of his kingdom. To try to bring to an end these devastating clan feuds, among other measures he appointed Ludovic, Duke of Lennox, to take appropriate action within the Shires of Dumbarton and the Lennox dukedom. The Duke ordered that certain landlords find cautioners that they would be answerable to justice over grievances. Sir Patrick Maxwell, John's grandfather, became his cautioner, and David Cunningham of Ibert, Walter Leckie of Easter Poldar and William Graham of Doucheall became cautioners for Malcolm MacFarlane of Gartartan, to appear before the Duke 'to make redress for the enormities for which they were answerable.'

The reputation of the MacFarlanes generally was not helped at this time by the believed participation of the Chief's son, John, in the Battle of Glen Fruin on 7th January 1603. The Colquhouns had the misfortune to be in a state of hostility, not only towards the MacFarlanes but also with the MacGregors. This particular feud culminated in a clash of arms in Glen Fruin. John MacFarlane and Dougall MacCoull MacFarlane of Drumfad and Tullichintaul were also later accused of involvement. It was this battle that led to the MacGregors being declared rebels at law, with disastrous results for their Clan. At the battle some theological students who had inadvisedly come out from Glasgow to witness the fight were themselves massacred, and the blame fell upon the MacGregors. There was, however, a tradition among the MacFarlanes that the perpetrators of this savage crime were a certain Donald Lean and his servant Charlioch. Justice caught up with these two later, for on taking refuge in MacFarlane territory they assaulted two women, one of whom managed to stab the servant. The wound delayed their escape and they were hunted down by the MacFarlanes and killed.

It was soon after this, in 1608, that the MacFarlanes were themselves declared rebels at law. It would be reasonable to believe that it was this severe penalty that led to conciliation with the Colquhouns. The feud certainly ended, for we know that MacFarlanes supported the Colquhouns against the MacGregors when the King ordered justice to fall upon that Clan. The feud then was over, but in January 1610, as an individual, John MacDouill Vic Neill MacFarlane was denounced as a rebel and put to the horn for not finding sufficient caution for his personal appearance to answer for the murder of Catherine Gillemor.

In 1611 or 1612 the old Chief, Andrew, died and was buried in Luss churchyard. John, his successor and fifteenth Chief, erected a stone over his father's grave. The stone is carved with a death's head and an hour-glass with crossbones on one side and a crossed scythe and spade on the other. The translated inscription runs:

Here is the burial place
Appointed for the Lairds
of Arroquhar, buildit by Johne
MackFarlan Laird thereof

Efter deathe
Remainis Vartew
Memento Mori
    J.M. 1612

So Andrew, who had been Chief for approximately sixty-five years, was laid to rest.

XVII
The Plantation of Ulster

A nother event of great significance to the MacFarlanes took place during Andrew's time as fourteenth clan Chief. This has become known as the 'Plantation of Ulster'. We have already seen that from AD 500–800 there was a Dalriadic Kingdom of the Scots in Western Scotland, founded by the fierce tribe of the Scots from Northern Ireland, and undoubtedly through the centuries there was travel in both directions. After Bannockburn in 1314, Robert Bruce and his brother made a military excursion into Ireland through Ulster, and for centuries Scots had come to Ireland and settled there. It has been noted that John MacFarlane, the brother of the ninth Chief, Walter, had founded a family in Northern Ireland in the fifteenth century.

What is known as the Plantation of Ulster was of a different nature, more in line with a deliberate political policy, such as had been attempted previously, with little success. The object was to stabilize English government and law in Northern Ireland; some called it colonising and others civilising. The native people were regarded as wild, undisciplined and lawless, and it was believed that this could be changed for the better by settling more lawful and civilised people in their midst. It had been tried in what were known as King's and Queen's Counties in 1550, in Ulster in 1570, in Munster in 1560 and 1580. Those who were dispossessed by the arrival of these strangers naturally proved very hostile. In fact there was too little money and support for these ventures to be a success.

In 1606 two Scottish adventurers, Montgomery and

Hamilton, made a deal with a Gaelic Chieftain for a settlement in his territory. This proved successful, and through this piece of land many individual settlers made their way into Ulster generally. Most of them were Scottish Presbyterians who had as much reason to move out of the reach of the English as their Roman Catholic compatriots.

Between 1608 and 1610 there followed a systematic attempt to settle people from both England and Scotland in the counties of Donegal, Tyrone, Derry, Armagh, Cavan and Fermanagh, and by 1622 there were some thirteen thousand newcomers. When the settlement actually began, fifty-nine out of the seventy Scots who had come forward were accepted. Among them were five nobles, the Duke of Lennox (second Duke and seventeenth Earl), his brother Lord D'Aubigny (Esme Stewart, later to be third Duke and eighteenth Earl), the Earl of Abercorn, the Lord of Burley, and Lord Ochiltree (whose daughter, we remember, was the first wife of Duncan MacFarlane, thirteenth Chief). Many of these settled in County Tyrone. Thus it has come about that there were many MacFarlanes in Ireland and through them, by emigration, in North America, Canada, Australia and New Zealand.

The Duke of Lennox mentioned above made a promise of two hundred men and nominated Andro Dow of Gartartan to be Captain. These troops formed part of a force of two thousand men to be sent to Ireland by an Order of the Lords of Council, dated 1602. Perhaps some of the settlers came from the Gartartan area in South Perthshire. Within the eighty-one thousand acres of land made available for the settlers in Northern Ireland would have been some MacFarlanes whose activities it is hoped in due course to discover and elucidate. It is known that those who had been dispossessed in the interests of plantation by no means accepted it meekly. There was, for example, a ferocious attack in 1641 made by Gaelic Irish Roman Catholics full of the kind of well authenticated atrocities which have bedevilled Irish history.

71

XVIII
Rough Times

From 1612 to 1624, John was the fifteenth Chief of Clan MacFarlane and an awesome character he must have been. We have already seen something of his personality as displayed by his hasty temper and fierce physical reactions in hostilities with other clans.

John married as his first wife, Susanna, a daughter of George Buchanan of that Ilk. This family, like the MacFarlanes, received the charter for their lands from the Earls of Lennox. Their territory lay on the east side of Loch Lomond. It does not appear to have been a happy marriage for they were subsequently divorced. They had had no children. It is possible that this divorce, or perhaps the lady's interest in Sir Humphrey Colquhoun, initiated a feud with the Buchanans which, by 1619, had escalated to the point where they were virtually at war. In this strife MacFarlane was supported by John Darleith, Lindsay of Balliol, Bunten of Ardoch, Galloway in Kilmaronock, the Drummonds and, strangely enough, the Colquhouns.

John's second marriage was to Lady Helen Stewart, a daughter of Francis, Earl of Bothwell. This Earl, known as the 'mad-cap' Earl, was a nephew of the Earl of Bothwell who was Mary Queen of Scots' third husband. John and Helen had a son, Walter, who became the next Chief. For his third wife, John married Elizabeth Campbell of Argyll who gave him four sons: Duncan, who, as we shall see was a most wild and unruly person and gave his father nothing but trouble – he did not marry; next, there was Andrew of Drumfad; then John, the ancestor of the MacFarlanes of Glen

Falloch; and finally George, the ancestor of the Clachan branch. John's fourth and final marriage was to Margaret, a daughter of James Murray of Strowan, who is believed to have been a very religious woman. They had no children.

Despite the making and breaking of truces, matters had not yet been settled financially between the MacFarlanes and the Colquhouns, for we find that on 13th June 1614, John, Earl of Mar, became surety for John MacFarlane of Arrochar, that he would appear at the next Justice-Aire in Dumbarton to answer for the crimes already mentioned. With him in the indictment was named Dougall MacCoull MacFarlane. The charge was the usual thing – the lifting of Colquhoun cattle from the lands of Glen Mulloche, Immerstachin and Drum Macnilling in June 1602 and also in the same year, from Glen Finlas, as many as six score cattle and oxen. The injured parties were named as Alexander Colquhoun of Luss, John Laing, Thomas McGilfadrick and Patrick Colquhoun.

There were also unsavoury matters with which the Chief had to contend, one of which led to the banishment from his home of his son Duncan. There are two accounts of the trouble that led to the Chief calling his son 'Black Duncan': one is given by the Rev. James Dewar, and the other by the Rev. H. S. Winchester. Dewar states that the matter began with a raid instigated by the Regent Athol and carried out by his men. This raid was one of several such raids upon the Arrochar territory. On this occasion they captured MacFarlane cattle and drove them away. John, the Chief, was at home at Eilean-a-Vow and saw that the enemy had superior numbers, so he decided to wait for a more suitable moment to attack. However, Duncan would not wait but, rowing from the island, landed and collected together a MacFarlane force. After a skirmish the Athol men retired to a MacFarlane hunting lodge at Grianach some three miles from Loch Sloy where they then rested. They were foolish enough to start celebrating with feasting and merry-making without placing sentries. Duncan and his men crept up, secured the doors, and then set fire to the house, killing all the occupants. Winchester's account adds that the fire grew out of control and caught hold of the heather and then the forest. By the time it had finished, there was left scarcely 'a tree standing or a tuft of heather between Loch Sloy and Garabal marsh'. Duncan then returned home and told his father what had happened. The Chief was both appalled and furious and, calling him 'Black Duncan of the mischief', banished him from home with the words: 'a bloody son you'll be to me', for he knew that one day Athol men would return for vengeance. Sir William Fraser states that this is indeed exactly what happened. Three Athol men came searching for Duncan and, without knowing who it was, suddenly came upon him while he was splitting wood on Eileen-a-Ghoar, an island in Loch Lomond. He said he would tell them where Duncan was if they would help him with a piece of wood. Suddenly knocking out a wedge he trapped their hands in the wood and then killed them.

Another indication of the kind of person Duncan was, is seen in one of his black deeds in Glen Loin. A party of men were driving cattle up the glen and came to a place near the ford of Coire-Ghroggain, where in those days the territory demanded that they should stoop down to go through an archway formed by two huge stones. As each one came through Duncan struck off their head and dragged the body clear for the next one to emerge.

The Chief had more trouble when, on 6th June 1623, Robert and Thomas MacFarlane accused George and John Buchanan of Gartincaber; Patrick, son of George Buchanan of Auchmar; John Beg Buchanan of Ballindewar and John, his son; Thomas Buchanan of Drougie, and Archibald, his brother, of the murder of their brother Duncan MacFarlane of Kippienoche in Drummond in the Lennox. The Chief appeared with Mr David Primrose, the advocate, to support Robert at the trial. The defence claimed that Duncan's father, Andrew Moir MacFarlane, was a notorious villain and that William Buchanan had traced some thefts in the Lennox to MacFarlane who, with his son Duncan and others, waylaid

Buchanan while he was on his own and, tying him to a tree, tortured him with stab wounds until he died. For this terrible crime they had been put to the horn but had continued in their evil ways. The accused had then pursued these culprits, Andrew and Duncan, and had killed them. The Lords ordered that the petitioners make an offer to the Laird of MacFarlane and all stay in Edinburgh until the matter be settled.

In February 1622 John MacFarlane of Arrochar, with the consent of his son and heir, Walter, sold to Andrew MacFarlane, son of Andrew McCoull MacFarlane of Blair Vyok, 'without reversion, and confirmed to him the lands of Gortane, in the lordship and barony of Luss, parish of Roseneath, and shire of Dumbarton, to be held of the granter and his heirs-male.' (MacFarlane 1922)

In 1624, some MacFarlanes were not bringing honour to their name. Some were found guilty of theft. Some were pardoned but, for some, their crimes were sufficiently serious for them to be moved out of their home lands to places in Aberdeenshire and Banffshire, where they assumed different surnames such as Stewart, McCondy, Greisck, MacInnes and MacJames. These are all names of Septs of Clan MacFarlane.

That there was another side to the character of the fifteenth Chief can be seen in that he built and endowed an almshouse at Bruitford on the mainland opposite his castle on Eilean-a-Vow. The purpose of the almshouse was to look after people who needed shelter while travelling in the district. This project may well have originated in the heart of his wife, Margaret, but he carried it out. On the front of the building he placed armorial bearings, with party per pale, baron and femme, three mullets (being the arms of Margaret Murray, his fourth wife). In the early 1900s the wall tracks of this building could still be traced at a place called Crutyforst (*Croit a' phuirt* in Gaelic, meaning 'the croft of the landing place').

XIX

A Royalist

Before looking at some of the events of Walter's chieftainship, the sixteenth of the Clan (to which he succeeded in 1624), we must look back a little to the historical scene in Scotland.

In the year 1603, James VI of Scotland, through the death of Queen Elizabeth I of England, became James I of England. This happened because his great-grandmother, Margaret, was a daughter of Henry VII, and Henry VIII had left no successors.

James came only once to Scotland after taking the throne of England, and his main interest in Scotland was to make sure that its church remained Episcopalian. While in the country he had tried to rule with strength and justice, and being no great lover of the nobility had tried to keep their wilder excesses within bounds. After going to England his zeal for Scottish affairs lessened somewhat, and his efforts at uniting the two countries both in politics and religion were not very successful. Although he could not bring the two countries under one parliament, he was able to create a single citizenship. Perhaps with good long-term results there was introduced compulsory education for the eldest sons of the Chiefs, to reduce what was believed to be their somewhat barbaric outlook on life. It was also made illegal to carry arms, although this had only a limited effect. More successfully, Chiefs were required to appear from time to time to answer for illegalities committed by members of their clan. Such efforts may well have disposed the people of MacFarlane's turn of mind to be favourably inclined towards the King.

James was succeeded in 1625 by his son, Charles I, and Scotland did not take kindly either to her new King nor to his ideas about kingship, still less to his views about the nature of the Church. In particular, his orders about the kind of liturgy that must be used in worship aroused great opposition, so much so that, in 1638, people all over Scotland signed what was known as the 'National Covenant'. In this, they repudiated the new form of liturgy and any perpetuation of what was thought to be the ways of Rome. So strongly was this covenant supported that the people went on to demand a free parliament and a free general assembly. Meanwhile, the King was also becoming increasingly unpopular in England.

In Scotland, the Covenanters gradually became divided among themselves. While all wanted what later became known as Presbyterianism as their form of Church order, some also wanted increasingly to restrict the power of the King. Argyll was a keen Covenanter and so, at the outset, was Montrose, who had been made a Marquis by the King; but later, though still believing in the Presbyterian system, his views on kingship brought him back to the King's side. The Covenanters, wanting to assist parliament against the King, sent a force under the command of David Leslie, whose aid was to prove a contributory factor in the defeat of the King. However, Montrose now decided to try to bring Scotland back to allegiance to their King.

Walter MacFarlane gave his loyalty to his King and joined Montrose in his struggles in the years 1644 and 1645. Montrose had a whole series of victories and, after taking Aberdeen in 1644, he moved successfully about the country. At Inverlochy he defeated his old enemy Argyll in his own lands near Fort William in Inverness-shire. Walter would almost certainly have been in this battle at Inverlochy. Perhaps on this occasion would have been heard the pibroch, 'Thogail nam Bò'. Whether the Clan badge, the cranberry, or cloudberry, would have been clearly enough seen to have united his men amidst all the bustle and fighting, the cry,

'*Loch Sloy*' must have been raised many times. Walter was eventually fined three thousand Scots marks for joining Montrose, and twice he was beseiged in his castle on Inveruglas by Cromwell's men. Ultimately, the castle was taken and destroyed together with many family papers. It is now a lonely, sad, and beautiful little ruin.

One of the gentlemen of the bedchamber to James VI was Sir James Semple of Beltrees in Renfrewshire, who had also been Scottish Ambassador in England in 1599. He had a daughter, Margaret, whom Walter married. They had two sons and one daughter. John succeeded his father as seventeenth Chief, and, as he had daughters, he was himself succeeded by his brother, Andrew of Ardess. John's sister, Giles, married Adam Colquhoun of the Glens.

If MacFarlane had to suffer for his loyalty to his King, so too did his neighbour at Rossdhu. In 1653 William, Earl of Glencairn, was Commander-in-Chief of the Royalist forces in Scotland, and he had given a commission to John Dennistoun of Colgrain who was defending Rossdhu. When Dennistoun marched out to go north with the Lennox Fencibles (among whom there would certainly have been some MacFarlanes), Lt. Col. Cottrell captured the castle for Cromwell. Under the leadership of the Laird of MacNaughton and the eldest son of Sir George Maxwell of Newark (a family with whom the MacFarlanes were related by marriage as we have already seen), the Royalists recaptured the castle. Once more it changed hands when Col. Cooper won it again for the Cromwellians. After the resignation of the Earl of Glencairn, General Middleton commanded the Royalists. He came to Rossdhu on a recruiting drive. Later he was defeated by the Cromwellians at Lochnair.

As a result of following Montrose, some MacFarlanes adopted the Grahams of Montrose as their Chief and settled in Buchanan in Stirlingshire. The link with the Grahams is seen in the burial ground on Inchcailloch in Loch Lomond, where the tombstones reveal that many Grahams and

MacFarlanes lived in the same area. Some MacFarlanes kept the boatyard at Balmaha for seven generations. One stone relating to a Duncan MacFarlane of Inchfade bears the MacFarlane arms.

There is a story in Sir F. Dick Lander's book, *Wanderings in the Highlands*, about the burning of MacFarlane's Forest, an area of some twenty-five miles round extending from Loch Lomond to Ben Laoigh. The event is believed to have taken place when Walter was Chief. It seems that Walter had a shepherd named Angus MacFarlane who was betrothed to a girl called Ellen. She told the Laird of a dream she had had of the forest being on fire, and of the Laird carrying Angus's body. That evening Lochaber men raided MacFarlane's cattle and were traced to a hut in the forest. When the Laird set fire to it to flush them out, the fire burnt out of control and took hold of the forest. A large tree fell and killed Angus, so the girl's dream came true when she saw the Laird carrying Angus' body out of the forest. Overcome with grief, she is believed to have fallen down and died.

After reading so much about the MacFarlanes being involved in many violent and martial occasions, it is interesting to know of the Chief being concerned in church matters. The Minister of Luss, a Mr McLauchlan, had apparently been guilty of some irregularities, one of which was to have married Sir John Colquhoun, sixteenth Chief of Luss, to Margaret Baillie, without fulfilling the legal necessity of calling banns. The upshot of his behaviour was that he was deposed from office on 26th December 1648. On January 23rd 1649, the Covenant was renewed in Luss parish church, the Laird having been advised to have the people of Arrochar present. The Presbytery of Dumbarton has the following entry in its minute book:

Mr David Elphinstone [was] to preach before noon, and Mr Archibald McLean [was to preach in the] afternoon, in the Irish language and betwixt the sermons the said Mr David and Mr John Stewart are... to read the solemn engagement and Covenant... on the Sabbath thereafter, and Gillish McArthur, Clerk to the Session, is ordained to have the parishioners duly advised to keep the Fast at the said kirk, and especially to advise the Laird of MacFarlane to have his people of the Arrochar present, and the said Mr David to intimate the vacancy of the place.

It was during Walter's time that it was suggested that the spiritual needs of the four hundred people in the area could be better met with a church, a minister and glebe at Arrochar because Luss parish church was some ten miles away. The Dumbarton Presbytery supported by both MacFarlane and Sir James Colquhoun put in a petition to this effect to the Council of Estates who, on 24th December 1658, ordered Robert Hamilton of Barnes to call together interested parties in the dismemberment of land from Luss parish, and in the creating of a new church at Tarbet with a manse and glebe for the minister and, if there was general agreement, to bring the project into effect. In the event, a site was chosen and the Presbytery made a perambulation of the parish, but no further progress was made for ten years. The long delay seems strange when there was so much agreement. Sir John Colquhoun had subscribed a bond on January 25th 1659

> to denude himself of the sum of 400 merks yearly, payable by the Laird of MacFarlane for the tithes of his lands of Arrochar and fifteen bolls teind meal, payable forth of the lands in Arrochar (Stuckgown) belonging to Walter MacFarlane of Gartartan, in favour of the minister of Tarbet and his successors in all time coming, and to be uplifted by the first minister after his entry to the ministry at Tarbet.

Moreover, the heir of Arrochar, John MacFarlane, was also agreeable to the division of Luss parish, and pledged himself to build a church with a manse for the minister and to give a 'competent' glebe.

Perhaps MacFarlane later had second thoughts – the old church at Luss had been sufficient for his forefathers. If public worship had not figured in his life to any significant degree, the whole matter may have seemed relatively unimportant to him. At any rate the delay continued so long that another perambulation was made in 1676 eight years after Walter, the sixteenth Chief, had died.

XX
Regal and Religious Tensions

It was not long after the victory of Cromwell's men at Naseby in 1645 that Charles I placed himself with the Scottish forces. As he was unwilling to allow the Scots to have the Presbyterianism they wanted, they gave him up to the English, only to discover that the English were no more ready to accede to their wishes than the King had been. Because of this, some of them wanted to have the King back again and were ready to rescue him if he would grant their wishes. Other more rigid Covenanters, however, set their minds against this.

When the rescue army under the Marquis of Hamilton was defeated by Cromwell in Lancashire, it remained for those who had been against the King in Scotland to resolve matters with Cromwell. They found him to be totally intractable, and when the King was executed in 1649 they were outraged.

Wanting a King, the Scots chose the King's son (Charles II), who was only eighteen at the time and living in Holland. He, like his father, was not really in favour of the Covenant, so he tried to win back the crown before giving them his answer. He did not undertake the necessary military efforts himself but sent the Marquis of Montrose. The Marquis could not repeat his former military successes and was defeated in his first battle at Carbisdale in Sutherland in April 1650. He was taken and later executed. Cromwell followed this up by defeating a Scots army led by David Leslie at the Battle of Dunbar in the same year. In 1651 Charles' army was so decisively beaten at the Battle of Worcester that he was forced to escape to France where he remained in exile.

He made another attempt to win back the crown when he sent General Middleton, but he too was defeated at Dalsnaspidal near Loch Garry. It seems that, when General Monck was left behind in Scotland to bring the country to heel, he had done his job only too well.

In 1658 Cromwell died and his son, Richard, thought that the time had come for the restoration of the monarchy and so, on May 25th 1660, Charles II landed back in England to the satisfaction of most of his people. It did not help him that he stayed away from Scotland and tried to rule through a Privy Council, nor that he firmly restored Episcopacy. The people continued to feel strongly about religious matters and they did not hide their opinions or their feelings. Thus the struggle went on. When the King appointed the Earl of Lauderdale as Secretary to the Council, the Earl decided that the Covenanters who refused to acknowledge Charles as their King, and to accept Episcopacy into their church life, would be compelled to do so. This conflict led to a particularly unhappy time for Scotland.

Charles II died in 1685. He was succeeded by James II, his brother, who being a Roman Catholic, attempted to impose this faith on Scotland once more. In practical terms it meant even fiercer persecution of the Covenanters, many of whom were killed and many others sent as slaves to the plantations in the Americas.

In these wider matters concerning Scotland's history the MacFarlanes were again involved. A detachment of MacFarlanes was in the Duke of Monmouth's army at the Battle of Bothwell Bridge in 1679. The Covenanters had said before the battle that they would lay down their arms if the King would grant Scotland a free Parliament and a free Assembly, but Monmouth would not agree to this and in the ensuing battle some four hundred Covenanters were killed and twelve hundred taken prisoner. Those who were ready to sign a bond not to take up arms against the King were allowed to go home. The two hundred and ten who refused to sign were sentenced to be shipped to Barbados to become slaves. Unfortunately, most of them lost their lives when they were shipwrecked off Orkney.

Walter Scott refers to the MacFarlanes at Bothwell Bridge in *Old Mortality* when he writes:

> The defence made by the Covenanters was so protracted, and obstinate, that the royal generals began to fear that it might be successful. While Monmouth threw himself from his horse, and rallying the Foot Guards, brought them on to another close and desperate attack, he was warmly seconded by General Thomas Dalziel, who, putting himself at the head of a body of Lennox Highlanders, rushed forward with their tremendous war cry, '*Loch Sloy*'.

At this point we must refer to Loch Sloy for it held a special significance for Clan MacFarlane. Loch Sloy may be approached from Glen Loin at the head of Loch Long. It is a remote and large loch nestling under the great heights of Ben Vane and Ben Vorlich, about one mile long and a quarter of a mile wide. It was the place where the MacFarlanes rallied before going out to meet their enemies, and to which they retired when their foes were too strong for them. The name Loch Sloy appears in a compartment of the Chief's Arms, and it was used as the Clan's battle cry. In 1950 Queen Elizabeth, the Queen Mother, opened the power station which was connected to Loch Sloy when a dam was built across one end of the loch, raising the water some one hundred and fifty feet and channelling it to the generating station at Inveruglas.

We return to our Clan story. John MacFarlane, the seventeenth Chief, married twice. His first wife was Grizel, a daughter of Sir Colin Lamond of that Ilk and Beatrice, a daughter of Lord Semple. John and Grizel had three daughters: Jean, who married John Buchanan of Lenie in 1666; Giles, who married Alexander M'Millan of Dunmore; and Grizel, who married Archibald Buchanan of Torie in 1673. John's second wife was Anne, a daughter of Campbell of Duntroon. She was the widow of the Captain of the Carrick. This marriage presented John with three more daughters. He is believed to have died in 1679, but the date is uncertain.

We have already seen that John had been involved in the matter of a new church at Tarbet, even if it proved to be in a somewhat desultory way. But this must not lead us to suppose that these were peaceful and settled times. We learn from the rents of the Barony of Luss that the MacDonalds were on the war-path threatening the area. Sir James Colquhoun at his own expense sent a 'policing' force to the head of Loch Long. The actual entry runs as follows:

> Item, to allow to the compter his expenses in going with a number of men to the head of Loch Long to protect the country, at the time of the MacDonalds, at the Laird's special command £40

> Item, paid to John Colquhoun, officer at the Laird's command for his own and two men's charges at the head of Loch Long, 10 days time, keeping the country £10

The fact that it was the Laird Colquhoun and not the Laird MacFarlane who met this financial responsibility may indicate that at this time (1679) the Colquhouns were growing stronger in power and influence in the region. Certainly when Sir James Colquhoun received from the Commissioners of Frances, Duchess of Lennox (the widow of Charles, Duke of Lennox), further grants of land, some of which (such as Drumfad and Tullichintaul) had belonged to the Dougal MacFarlane whose father had been killed by Sir Humphrey Colquhoun, clearly the Colquhouns' power was growing.

XXI
The Last Warrior Chiefs

We have seen that from his two marriages, John, the seventeenth Chief of Clan MacFarlane, had six daughters; so it came about that the title passed to his brother, Andrew of Ardess. Seven years before he became Chief, Andrew had declared his coat of arms at the Heraldry Office in Edinburgh. There were differences between his version and the original one. The demi-savage in the original had a sheaf of arrows in his right hand, whereas Andrew's arms showed the demi-savage holding a sword.

Andrew, the eighteenth Chief, married twice. His first wife was Elizabeth, a daughter of John Buchanan of Ross and Drumakill. She gave him two sons – John, his heir who became the nineteenth Chief, and Walter who did not marry. Andrew's second wife was Jean Campbell of Strachan, who gave him five sons. Sadly, three sons of this second marriage fell in one battle. They were fighting against the French in the War of the Spanish Succession, at the Battle of Malplaquet on September 11th 1709, which resulted in great losses on both sides. Andrew, who was a major, and his brothers Archibald and Walter all died leaving no family. Of the other two brothers, William married a daughter of Govan of Buchapel and they had no children; Duncan, an army captain, married a French lady and they had two sons. The elder of these (James) married a Jean Forbes, who was a daughter of Sir Alexander Forbes of Foveran. The younger son (Duncan) went to Jamaica as a businessman. Whether he married there or not is not known.

It has been stated above that the three brothers who fell at

Malplaquet left no children, but it must be said that the Hunston family in Ireland base their claim to the MacFarlane chieftainship on the grounds that their ancestor, Malcolm, was a nephew of John MacFarlane the nineteenth Chief. We do not know who this Malcolm was but, to have been the Chief's nephew, his father must have been either Archibald or Walter. There is no evidence as yet that either was married.

Andrew, the eighteenth Chief, was predeceased by his son, John, on 9th July 1705, but John had exercised the powers of that office from about 1685. He came to the notice of the King when James II, in his efforts to ensure law and order, made use of powerful people in the various Scottish districts. John, with four hundred men at his command, was ordered to keep the peace in Renfrewshire. This was a responsibility he did not like. It may have been for political or financial reasons, or perhaps both, but he retired from the task. It is not surprising therefore that after William and Mary had landed in England in 1688, three years after John had become Chief, he decided to give them his support. On May 11th 1689 the Scottish crown was offered to William and Mary, and King James fled to France. John Graham of Claverhouse, Viscount Dundee, raised an army to try to recover the throne for King James. John MacFarlane offered to raise a regiment himself to support the government, and he was made a Colonel of a Regiment of Foot, but his offer was not needed as Dundee was killed and his army defeated by William's army under General MacKay at the Battle of Killiecrankie, near Pitlochry, on July 27th 1689. A further battle fought at Dunkeld three weeks after Killiecrankie resulted in another defeat for the Highlanders, who this time were led by Colonel Cannon. There were no further engagements and the MacFarlanes did not have to take the field.

Clan MacFarlane's nineteenth Chief was married twice. Agnes, a daughter of Sir Hugh Wallace of Woolmot, was his first wife and they had a son who died young. John's second wife was Helen, a daughter of the second Viscount Arbuthnott, and they had four sons and a daughter. The eldest son, Walter, succeeded his father and became the twentieth Chief; Robert died young; William succeeded his brother to become the twenty-first Chief; Alexander became a merchant, and the daughter died young.

Alexander had been to Glasgow University and was well educated. Being a good mathematician he became interested in astronomy. In the pursuit of this interest he acquired some valuable instruments, which in his will he left to his university. They were repaired and set up by his celebrated relative, James Watt, in the University Observatory on Dove Hill which was named after MacFarlane. In his work as a trader in Jamaica, Alexander made a considerable fortune. His ability was recognised in that he became a member of the island's legislative assembly and also served as an assistant judge. When he died, unmarried, in 1775 Alexander left extensive estates including those at Large Island to his brothers Walter of Arrochar and William, who was a physician in Edinburgh.

John was responsible for the building of Inverioch House, near Tarbet, in 1697. There is a painting of this house originally in the possession of the Hunston House family in Ireland. During later extensions and rebuilding a stone was taken from the original house and placed over the front entrance of the present house, now the Cobbler Hotel. The stone has an inscription in Gaelic carved on it which roughly translated reads:

This stone was taken from the main entrance of the house built by John, Chief of the MacFarlanes and Laird of Arrochar, in the year inscribed upon it.

XXII

A Scholar Chief

By now we have noted that MacFarlanes have figured in history for their patriotism, their loyalty to the Crown, their religious convictions coupled, perhaps, with their light attachment to religious obligations and, at times, for their lawlessness and hard treatment of their enemies.

When Walter succeeded his father in 1705, becoming the twentieth Chief at the age of fourteen, he remained Chief until 1767, living in the reigns of four monarchs – Queen Anne, George I, George II and George III. It was a period which brought traumatic changes to Scotland and into the life of Clan MacFarlane.

Although the Highlanders had been defeated at Dunkeld, they were still restless. The Earl of Argyll had supported King William; therefore, almost automatically, those who hated him supported King James. William now determined to prevent any further rebellion in the Highlands, and ordered that the Chiefs should take an oath of allegiance to him by January 1st 1692. All had done this except MacDonald of Glencoe, who did actually take the oath but not until after the date. This led to the terrible massacre of his family in Glencoe perpetrated by their traditional enemies, the Campbells. This event has never been forgotten and at the time it both blackened William's name and incensed his enemies.

Further trouble came to many of Scotland's leading men for which William was also blamed. There were laws which excluded the Scots from trading with the English colonies through the East India and East Africa Companies. To overcome this restriction the Scots tried to set up their own colony on the Isthmus of Darien (or Panama) in 1698. Disease, lack of provisions, quarrelling among themselves, attacks from the Spaniards, and resistance from the English in the West Indies and the Americas made a colossal disaster of the whole enterprise, costing Scotland two thousand lives and over £2,000,000 of investment. Walter's father, John, had invested and lost £200 in this project.

Just before Walter became Chief, Queen Anne had come to the throne and the two countries became united under one parliament. A year later the Treaty of Union was passed, whereby the two countries became one kingdom to be called Great Britain. It was certainly due to the two countries pursuing different policies that the Darien scheme could not be a success. However, the Scots became more and more disenchanted with the union. They disliked the new tax system, the ordinary person specially objecting to the malt tax, which appeared to be a tax on the drink of the common man. Others became increasingly impatient at the long delays over the payment of money promised to off-set the losses in the Darien scheme. In religious matters there was irritation over the removal of the right to choose their own ministers by the congregations; and, of course, the Roman Catholics who looked for the return of the exiled son of King James strongly disapproved of the religious clauses in the treaty. Nine years after Walter became Chief there came the first attempt to restore James' heir, Prince Charles, to the throne of Scotland. The Jacobites did not want George I to succeed Anne and so, under the leadership of the Earl of Mar (an Erskine), on the pretext of a deer-hunt, some Highland Chiefs met and decided to raise the standard for Prince Charles. At the Battle of Sherriffmuir in 1715, in which the Prince had not appeared in time to exert any influence on the outcome, Mar was defeated by the Duke of Argyll and took refuge together with the Prince in France.

The failure of the '15 led to laws against the carrying of arms – a law which General Wade was entrusted to enforce,

Walter, 20th Chief of MacFarlane

and in the pursuit of which he initiated a road-building programme which left a permanent mark upon the Highlands. There was also a revival of the malt tax which had somehow always been avoided, and stronger measures were taken against smuggling. It is known that Rob Roy MacGregor was involved on the Prince's side, but there is no evidence that the MacFarlanes officially joined him.

Looking ahead to the 1745 rebellion there is a conflict of evidence. McIan states that three hundred MacFarlanes fought with the Prince, while MacKay expressly states that although they could raise that number of men they were definitely not on the Prince's side – 'At no time was there one half of the Highland Clans engaged on the Jacobite side. From the very beginning many of them were Covenanters and Whigs – Campbells, Grants of Strathspey, Colquhouns, Forbes, MacFarlanes, MacKays, MacNaughtons, Munros, Rosses, Sinclairs and Sutherlands.' Maybe the solution to this clash of opinion lies in the fact that there were other MacFarlanes than those at Arrochar who may have supported the Prince.

The Battle of Culloden in 1746 put an end to Prince Charles' efforts to regain the throne and also wrought a total change in the life of Scotland. George II's brother, the Duke of Cumberland, with great cruelty made sure that the Highlands would not rise again against the King. Many Scots were killed, nearly one thousand were banished to America and the West Indies, and changes were introduced which fundamentally altered the Highland way of life by destroying clan traditions and loyalties. Arms were forbidden as was the wearing of the Highland dress, and the Chiefs were not permitted to raise their clans for any warlike activity. This meant among other things the end of the practice of cattle 'lifting', and the equally obnoxious practice of 'blackmail' – that is to say compelling people to pay money to ensure that their cattle in transit were not 'lifted'.

These harsh measures were reinforced by an awesome oath taken in 1746 which ran as follows:

I A.B. do swear as I shall answer to God at the great day
of judgement, I have not, and shall not have in my
possession any gun, sword, or arms whatsoever, and
never use tartan, plaid or any part of the Highland garb;
and if I do so may I be accursed in my undertakings,
family, and property, may I never see my wife, nor
children, nor father, mother or relations; may I be killed
in battle as a fugitive coward, and lie without Christian
burial in a foreign land, far from the graves of my
forefathers and kindred; may all this come upon me if I
break my oath.

Clearly any oath-breaker was to be treated as a rebel. He
could not look for protection by his Chief. Now, in any case,
the role of the Chief was to change from being a private
warrior to a landowner in the modern sense. This, too,
operated against those who looked to him for paternal care.
Now, to make the land pay, there came the practice of 'the
clearances' with all the attendant misery and hardship for
those turned out of their homes to make way for more
profitable sheep farming. Thus the heart was taken out of
clan loyalties and obligations. Inevitably many people felt that
there must be a better and happier life in other countries, and
many thousands emigrated to Canada and the United States.

In the case of the MacFarlanes, their Chief at this time was
not a warrior but a scholar with a scholar's interests. His
mother, Lady Helen, it has been suggested, persuaded her
husband John to purchase the superiority of the Arrochar
estates, which meant freedom from feudal service, a kind of
life that was anyway on the way out. It may have cost as much
as £5000 but it made possible a new kind of life for the family.
Much of Walter's work (through which he became a highly
respected antiquary) would have taken him away from
Arrochar and, indeed, one of its ministers, the Rev. Alexander
MacFarlane, lampooned his chief in Gaelic verse for
introducing North-country farmers and their customs into
clan territory. He had a thirty thousand acre estate to manage.
One of his main innovations was to remove the service

obligation of the tenant towards his landlord. This now became a money sum and was included in the rent. Many sheep roamed on the Arrochar hills and the whole estate became more profitable.

When Walter was at home he proved to be hospitable. He entertained Tobias Smollett to dinner, and another writer tells of Walter being able to repeat by heart in Gaelic all the poems of Ossian. Perhaps it was when entertaining General Wade that something of MacFarlane's pride came out, for it is recorded by Dr Johnson that when General Wade addressed the chief as 'Mr MacFarlane', he is alleged to have replied: 'Mr MacFarlane may with propriety be many but I, and only I am MacFarlane.'

We know exactly what Walter looked like as there is a portrait of him engraved by W.B.D.D. Turnbull, which was presented to the Faculty of Advocates in Edinburgh by his nephew, Walter, in 1786. On a personal level, he is described by Sir Robert Douglas as 'a man of great benevolence, an agreeable companion, and a sincere friend.'

Walter was married to Lady Elizabeth Erskine, a daughter of Alexander, the sixth Earl of Kellie, on 23rd April 1760; she was twenty-eight years younger than he. Elizabeth's mother, Janet, was the wife of Dr Archibald Pitcairn, a Jacobite. The age discrepancy caused scurrilous comment from James Boswell, Dr Johnson's biographer. His views seem to have been coloured by his own jaundiced view of women. At any rate Walter had companionship and help with his responsibilities in the estate. They had no children.

Reference must be made to the Chief's great reputation as a scholar. Of the soundness and scope of his erudition there can be no doubt when it is commented upon by such people as Sir Robert Douglas, the historian Skene, Sir Arthur Mitchell, Sir William Fraser, and the editors of Anderson's Diplomata Scotae (1739), Mr Anderson and Mr Thomas Riddiman; in this work they paid generous tribute to the help he had given them. The Chief's reputation arose from his careful work as an antiquarian. Donald Whyte's book, *Walter*

MacFarlane, Clan Chief and Antiquary, published in 1988 refers fully to his manuscripts which covered such topics as genealogy, geography and translations of religious charters.

It was during Walter's chieftainship that Tarbet Church was at last built. It had been authorised in 1709 and was built in 1733. The manse was not erected for another one hundred years, and we have seen some of the suggested reasons why there was this long delay. To them must be added, perhaps, the youth of the Chief at first, and subsequently his financial position. In 1742, the Chief's widowed mother, Lady Helen, married John Spottiswoode of that Ilk, and was able from her secure financial position to help her son by renouncing some of the rental due to her from the MacFarlane estate.

Lady Helen presented Communion chalices to Arrochar Church. These are engraved with the Arbuthnott crest – a peacock's head on a wreath, couped proper and with the following inscription: 'The gift of the Honourable Helen Arbuthnott to the Parish of Arroquhar.' She also gave two hundred merks for the purchase of a bell for the church and another five hundred for the poor of the parish. In 1745 Walter granted an obligation dated 3rd September at Tarbet, to the minister and other members of the Kirk Session at Arrochar, for the two hundred merks his mother had given, with the interest from the term of Whitsunday 1742. He also granted bills for the payment of the other sum. In the event, neither of these legacies were paid for many years – indeed, not until after Walter's death.

We have noted that Walter and Elizabeth had no children, and so when he died on April 3rd 1767 in Edinburgh after seven years of marriage, the chieftainship passed to his brother William, who was living and working as a doctor in Edinburgh. Walter was buried in Greyfriars Church, which has since been rebuilt. Building projects frustrated the author's attempts to track down the home in which Walter and Lady Elizabeth lived.

XXIII

The Passing of an Inheritance

William, the twenty-first Chief, succeeded his brother in 1767, inheriting responsibilities for the legacies which were still to be honoured, as well as for the estates which he was to hold for some seventeen years; but he was to be the last Chief to hold the traditional clan lands at Arrochar.

As a doctor in Edinburgh William had his own life to live and it was a very different one from some of his more turbulent forefathers. Sentimentalists might regret the passing away of the old powers, but not all took that view. The Rev. John Gillespie, writing of Arrochar in 'The Old Statistical Account of Scotland' in 1790, states that: 'the people of this parish are mostly MacFarlane, and until lately, they have always had a strong attachment to the Laird as Chief; and while this subsisted, misanthropy and ferocity were marked features in their character." The Minister may well have been right in his assessment, but at least he recognised that alongside the less agreeable ferocity there was the loyalty which we have already noted more than once in our story. A more serious aspect of the matter was the atrophy of the protective paternalism which, despite all its faults, was at some periods of history the only protection for the weak and disadvantaged members of the community. For such people the Chief was becoming increasingly remote. For the MacFarlanes of Arrochar, the Chief now lived in Edinburgh.

It seems that William was not over-wise in money matters, choosing to live a life style that was of greater luxury than he could afford, and included driving round Edinburgh in a coach-and-four. This extravagance was exacerbated by unsuccessful attempts at gambling. Some of William's journeys round the city took him to a businessman named Parlane MacFarlane, from whom he ordered two china tea-sets. One set he gave to Parlane, although it is not known who this Parlane was. Parlane's son, on visiting the Chief's eldest daughter, Janet, and her niece, Margaret, who lived together, was presented with a cup and saucer from one of the original sets. It is said that there are other pieces from these sets in the hands of other members of the family. [See also the back cover illustration.]

William was married to Christian Dewar, a daughter of James Dewar of Vogrie, and they had three sons and three daughters who survived childhood. Of his daughter, Janet, there is more to tell, but nothing is known of Helen and Rachel. John, the eldest son, although he predeceased his father, is reckoned to be the twenty-second Chief, the first of the landless chiefs of the clan. Walter, the second son, married Marion, a daughter of John Trotter of Morton Hall and had five children. Their first son, William, was born in 1769, and became a sailor and eventually a first mate on an East Indiaman commanded by the Hon. Captain Elphinstone. He died, unmarried, at St. Helena some time before 1811. The two daughters, Christian, born in 1770, and Janet, born in 1774, are believed to have trained as milliners in Edinburgh and then to have worked in London, where one of them is understood to have married a Mr Loch; of Alexander, the second son, we know nothing but his name.

Robert, Walter and Marion's youngest son, was born in 1780. At that time, the family was living at Fountain Bridge, Edinburgh and, before that, at Saughton Hall, also in Edinburgh. Robert married and had two sons and a daughter. The elder son and the daughter died young. The younger son joined the army and, while serving in India, developed sun-stroke; this so affected his mind that he had to go into a private asylum, where he lived for fifty-three years. Robert is known to have often stayed with his cousin, Francis, who founded an Irish branch of MacFarlanes.

William and Christian's third son was Robert, who became head of a school in Blackheath and a man of letters. He was the first to publish reports of debates in the Houses of Parliament, before Hansard, at a time when note-taking was forbidden. One tradition says that he had the misfortune to have been run over by a carriage in Hammersmith on August 8th 1804; others believe that he was alive in 1827.

In 1784, the Chief was overwhelmed by financial troubles. He tried to ease the situation by selling the estate in Jamaica that he had inherited from his brother, but the £8000 he received from this sale was insufficient, and so it came about that the lands which had been in his family for over six hundred years were put up for sale, and the estates of William and his son, John, were vested in trustees on behalf of their creditors. The sale of MacFarlane's estates on 7th July 1784 is recorded in *The Stirling Antiquary* as follows:

At the instance of Hugh Norman, eldest son and heir served and returned to the deceased Hugh Mossman, writer in Edinburgh, against, William MacFarlane, Esq. of MacFarlane, John MacFarlane Junior therof, and their creditors.

Rental of the lands and Barony of Arrochar and others in the Shire of Dumbarton.

DOWN – The half of the lands of Down – Malcolm MacFarlane and his mother lease of 21 years from Whitsunday, 1766, money rent £10 13s.

DOWN – The other half of Down, Peter and Donald MacIntyre, 19 years, 1768.

ARDLEISH – Ardleish, Dougal and Alexander MacDougals, now Malcolm MacFarlane, a stone of butter at the proven conversion of 10s is added to the money rent – 19 years.

BLAIRSTANG and STUCKMUD – Malcolm MacFarlane and Margaret Campbell.

GARVUAL – Margaret Lauder. After Whitsunday 1787, the rent rises to £42.

GARRACHIE and ARDLUIE – Alexander MacFarlane

Shicandroin.

UPPER ARDVORLICH.

UPPER INVEROUGLASS and forest of BEINVEURLIC and NETHER ARDVOURLIC.

CAENMORE and BLAIREUNICH.

PART of TARBET called INVERCHULIN.

HILL of TARBET.

PART of TARBET called CLADDOCHBEG.

CLADDOCH mire with the laigh park of BALHENNAN.

COINLACH.

TYUNLOAN.

CLADDOCH.

ANOTHER PART of DITTO.

EASTER BALHENNAN.

Pendicle of BALHENNAN and HOUSE and WYND at TY VICHATTAN.

PART of BALHENNAN.

STUCHNACLOICH.

UPPER and NETHER STUCKINTIBBERT.

FIRKEN.

Mill of CAMBUSNACLACH and Mill Lands.

NETHER INVEROUGLASS.

CHOILCORRAN and INVERGROIN, GARTANFAIRED and GREITNEIN, expiration of present lease £88 4s. 9½d.

TYNALARACH ARDINNY and MUIRLAGAN.

STRONFYNE GLENLUYNS and the lands and mill of PORTCHIRBLE and hill of BEINVEIN.

TYNCLACH.

The Baron Officers sons pay for attune.

TULLICHENTAAL.

The tenant pays over and above his rent the stipend to the Minister of Luss, being 3 bolls meal, 8½ stone to the boll, and 40s. Scots, or 3s. 4d. of money and 3s. 1d. for Communion elements, and as the payment of stipend agrees with the teind duty in the feu charter to the superior, it is not here added to their rental nor is it hereafter stated as a deduction. The school salary being

4s. 3d., is also paid by the tenant over and above the rent. Stuckgown comprehending Stuckdon and Stuckvolge – George Syme, vassal, John Brock in Garshucke, and Archibald MacLachan, tacksman in Bunnackrae, both bred farmers and grassers concur in deponing that they both together visited and inspected the farms of Inveresk and Balfrone and parks about the mansion house of New Tarbet, all in the natural possession of MacFarlane, and that in their opinion they were worth upon a 19 years' lease of yearly rent £47 10s. 0d.

Fuller details regarding the sale may be found in James MacFarlane's *History of Clan MacFarlane* but the above list gives some idea of the extent of the estate. At the sale the estate was sold to a Mr Ferguson of Wraith for £28,000. It was sold again by his son, Robert, thirty-seven years later to Sir James Colquhoun of Luss for £78,000.

Alasdair Alpin MacGregor, writing in his book *Wild Drumalbain*, recounts the old tradition of 'an ominous black swan' which is associated with the loss of MacFarlane lands.

MacFarlane kept upon the upper waters of Loch Lomond a flock of white swans. Upon the well-being of this flock depended the fortunes of the House of Arrochar. Now, in the latter days of the last chief a seer named Robert MacPharrie pronounced that the family was nearing an end, and would become defunct soon after a wild black swan had taken up its abode with MacFarlane's white flock. In the course of time a black swan actually settled with the flock, and remained many weeks on Loch Lomond, shortly after which the Arrochar and Glen Falloch properties passed finally out of the hands of the MacFarlanes.

William, the twenty-first Chief, died at Bredisholme, Lanark, in 1787, and did not live to see the passing of his inheritance to the Chief of the clan with which his own clan had feuded so bitterly in the past. Nor could he possibly have envisaged that one day at the beginning of the nineteenth century his old home would begin a new life as a hotel.

William's death was nine years after the repeal of the 1746 Act which had done so much to destroy part of the clan tradition. The following proclamation is in translation from the Gaelic:

> This is bringing before all the sons of the Gael that the King and Parliament of Britain have for ever abolished the Acts against the Highland dress that came down to the clans from the beginning of the world to the year 1746. This must bring great joy to every Highland heart. You are no longer bound down to the unmanly dress of the Lowlander. This declaring to every man, young and old, Commons and Gentles, that they may after this put on and wear the trews, the little kilt, the doublet and the hose, along with the tartan kilt, without fear of the law of the land or the jealousy of enemies.

When George IV visited Edinburgh in 1822, the Chiefs wore the traditional dress, no doubt with immense pride, especially on official occasions.

It is clear that when John became the landless twenty-second Chief, the chieftainship was being emptied of its meaning for the MacFarlanes, since his father was alive in Edinburgh. As with so many others, the Clan was being deprived of the leadership it had known and respected or feared for many centuries, and with the loss of the ancestral lands there was beginning a new chapter in which those who bear the Clan name could wish that it might take yet another and happier turn

John married Catherine, a daughter of James Walkinshaw of that Ilk, and they had two sons and two daughters. There is no supporting evidence, but it is stated that the elder son, William, was born half-an-hour before his brother James, at Hermiston in the parish of Salton on May 29th 1770. Some believe that William emigrated to America, others that he only went there on a business trip. All that is known of James is that he was baptised at Arrochar.

William, then, was the twenty-third Chief in the direct line. We do not know who he married but he had a son, Walter, who also had a son, William, who died in 1866 without any family. Thus ended the direct line through the sons with William, the twenty-fifth Chief. John and Catherine's daughters were Margaret Elizabeth and Christian. Margaret was born in 1767 and went to live with her aunt Janet in Edinburgh, where she died, unmarried, on May 12th 1846. Christian also did not marry and died some time before her sister. If we are to look for a Chief, perhaps we should go back to William, the twenty-fifth Chief; he had a sister, Jane Watt, and it would have been in order for her to nominate someone. It is claimed that she did this 'in favour of a scion of the line of MacFarlane of Keithton.' There seems to be some doubt about whether the claim was formally taken up and recognised.

We now know that the last Chief's sister, Jane Watt (1817–1870), married a James Scott, an architect and builder, and had four children: Jean MacFarlan Scott, who was a draper in Sunderland; James Galbraith, who married a Janet Dunlop, a daughter of a shipmaster, John Dunlop; Walter MacFarlan Scott (1857–1927), also a draper in Sunderland, who married Isabella Robertson, nee Japp; and Sarah Galbraith. James and Janet had five children: James Galbraith, Mary Galbraith, John Dunlop (born 1886), Norman Craig (born 1892) and Douglas MacFarlan (born 1894). Walter and Isabella MacFarlan Scott had a daughter, Jane Watt (born 1897), who was alive in Sunderland in 1927.

Another interesting possibility regarding the chieftainship is in the line of the MacFarlanes of Hunston House, Co. Dublin, connected with the Francis referred to previously in this chapter. Other lines of enquiry are the MacFarlanes of Ardleish and the MacFarlanes of Muckroy and Erins. What MacFarlanes the world over would hope would be that the families in whom the Chief may be found will put their claims to the test with the Lord Lyon, for it would give immense pleasure to have the matter settled and loyalties to be firmly focused.

Returning to the sale of the estates in 1784, we remember that among the creditors was the Kirk Session. In fact, it was not until 1802 that the Session received the complete payment for the two hundred merks bequeathed by Lady Helen Arbuthnott in 1742. Thus it was sixty years after the bequest that the final payment was made. It was even longer before the money was spent on the purpose for which it was given.

In 1815, the minister, Mr Gillespie, reported to the Kirk Session that he had bought a bell from a Mr Brownlee of Greenock in October 1813 for £24 3s. 10d. The manse was not built until 1837, and the new church not until 1847. There being nowhere to hang the bell, it was put on a tree. While the bell was thus hung it proved to be a source of temptation to some people to 'have a pull'. There is a story of a certain Malcolm MacFarlane who, having been reproved by the Kirk Session over some matter, took his revenge by tying the bell-rope to the horns of Mrs Campbell's goat!

As might be expected from what we have heard about the people of Arrochar, they had less legal ways of entertaining themselves. Their minister during William's time (twenty-first Chief) was a Dr Stuart who is reported to have taken a sympathetic attitude towards their pleasures by warning some of his parishioners that excise men whom he met on the road were on the way. It was an area which in the nineteenth century saw the presence of the excise men frequently. There were shebeens, or unlicensed houses where liquor was sold, at eight places in the district – Tighvechtan, at Tarbet, three at Arrochar, one at Highlandman's Height, one at Glencroe school-house, and one at the Rest and be Thankful. The one at Highlandman's Height is believed to have been the house called Knockerbus by Robert Burns, and where he spent a night.

We have already seen (from his writings in *The Old Statistical Account of Scotland* (1790)) that the Rev. John Gillespie (Minister of Arrochar) saw such matters in a different light, believing that the sale of the estates, the going of the old chiefs, the making of military roads and the coming of the settlers from the low country 'contributed to extinguish the remains of that system of barbarity which so long retarded the civilisation of Europe. The people are now well-bred, honest and industrious, and not addicted to the immoderate use of spirituous liquors.' Perhaps he did not see what his parishioners did not want him to see.

Inverioch House, now The Cobbler Hotel

XXIV
Loyalty to a Name

It might seem that not knowing their Chief, nor possessing any longer the territories which were for so many centuries the heart-lands of the Clan, there remains no centre of loyalty for those who are called MacFarlane.

The role of the Chief has totally changed even where he or she can still be named among the clans. It may also seem right in these days of the redistribution of wealth that land should pass into other hands. Loyalties in Scottish terms, however, go deeper than that. It is natural for the heart to look to the rock from which it was hewn. Loyalty can find a focus elsewhere than in some vestigial feudalism.

Some MacFarlanes, like others from the Scottish clans, may have journeyed through life dishonourably; some humbly and obscurely; others courageously fighting and dying bravely. Some have won academic renown or athletic prowess; some have toiled on the land while others have carried their name all over the world on the high seas and left it in strange and distant places. If it is true that violence has been no stranger to them, it is also true that some have held high and humble responsibility in the service of the Gospel of Peace.

Some of the glory and some of the trouble which the Clan has known has undoubtedly come to them through their quality of loyalty. Perhaps it is this loyalty that will provide the dynamic for more historical research and also prove to be the uniting factor for all MacFarlanes.

Select Bibliography

Adam, Frank, *The Clans, Septs and Regiments of the Scottish Highlands*

Ashton, Robert, *James I by his Contemporaries*

Browne, James, *History of the Highlands*

Chadwick, Nora, *The Celts*

Eyre-Todd, George, *The Highland Clans of Scotland*

Gregory, Donald, *History of the Western Highlands and Isles of Scotland*

Fraser, Antonia, *James V King of Scots*

———, *King James VI of Scotland I of England*

Hastings, Max, *Montrose the King's Champion*

Hume Brown, P., *Scotland A Short History*

Kee, Robert, *Ireland*

MacFarlane, James, *History of Clan MacFarlane*

MacLean, Fitzroy, *A Concise History of Scotland*

MacKay, James, *William Wallace*

McLaren, Moray, *Scotland Shell Guide*

Munro, R.W., *Highland Clans and Tartans*

Murray, W.H., *Rob Roy MacGregor*

Nisbet, Alexander, *A System of Heraldry*

Prebble, John, *Culloden*

Salway, Peter, *Roman Britain*

Somerset-Fry, P. & F., *The History of Scotland*

Steel, Tom, *Scotland's Story*

Wain, John, *Samuel Johnson*

Whyte, Donald, *Walter MacFarlane, Clan Chief and Antiquary*

Appendix

Until comparatively recent times, members of a family were often designated 'so and so' son of 'so and so' son of 'so and so', which gave the descendants different branches of the family to which they could belong. There would be a main line connection, and there would be collateral relationships. The word 'sept' was often applied to branch families stemming from the main root. It was also used of unaffiliated families which had come under the protection of the main family.

A longer list of septs has been produced by Dr John Harris of the American MacFarlane Society.

MacFarlane Septs

	Shared with
Allan	MacDonald of Clanranald
Allanson	MacDonald of Clanranald
Bartholomes	Leslie
Caw	
Galbraith	MacDonald
Griesck	
Gruamach	
Kinnieson	
Lennox	Stewart
MacAindra	
MacAllan	MacDonald of Clanranald
MacCaa	
MacCause	
MacCaw	Stewart of Bute

MacCondy	
MacEoin	
MacGaw	
MacGeoch	
MacGreisich	Buchanan
Macinstalker	
Maclock	
MacJames	
MacKinlay	Buchanan, Farquharson, Stewart of Appin
MacNair	MacNauchton
MacNeur	
MacNider	
MacNiter	
MacRob	Gunn and Innes
MacRobb	
MacWalter	
MacWilliam	Gunn
Miller	
Monach	
Parlane	
Robb	
Stalker Thomason	Campbell
Weaver	
Weir	MacNauchton

Clan Badge

'Oireag' or Foighreag'	(Cloudberry)
'Muileag'	(Cranberry)

War Cry

'Loch Slòigh'	(Loch Sloy)
'The Loch of the Host'	

Clan Pipe Music

'Thogail nam Bò'	('Lifting the Cattle')
Spaidsearachd	(MacFarlane March)

APPENDIX

Designation of the Clan Chief
MacFarlane of that Ilk – MacPharlain, or MacPhatthaloin

Clan Precedence and the MacFarlane Arms
Derives from Baronage
Armorial Bearings 1646

The technical description of the Armorial Bearing in Lyon Register quoted from Frank Adam's *The Clans, Septs and Regiments of the Scottish Highlands* runs as follows:

> Arms: Argent, a saltire waved and cantoned with four roses gules. Crest, a demi-savage holding a sheaf of arrows in his right hand and pointing with his left to an imperial crown. Supporters, Two Highlanders in their native garb, armed with broadswords and bows proper (in the last matriculation they are blazoned 'brandishing their broadswords aloft' and stand on a compartment wavy).
>
> Mottos: over escutcheon, 'This I'll defend' and, under escutcheon, on a compartment wavy, 'Loch Sloy'.

There has been confusion about the MacFarlane Arms. Walter the twentieth Chief matriculated his Arms in 1750. The Citation in the Glasgow collection stated that 'this coat (of arms) has been worn by the ancestors of this family for several generations and was confirmed to them ... in the reign of Charles the First with this only variation that the Supporters were armed with bows and arrows instead of Broadswords.'

Walter the sixteenth Chief was Chief in Charles I's time. It is therefore the sword which should be in the hand of the demi-savage, and this has been so for over three hundred years.

Arms of Andrew of Ardess
Registered 1672

'Thogail nam bò theid sinn

Traditional

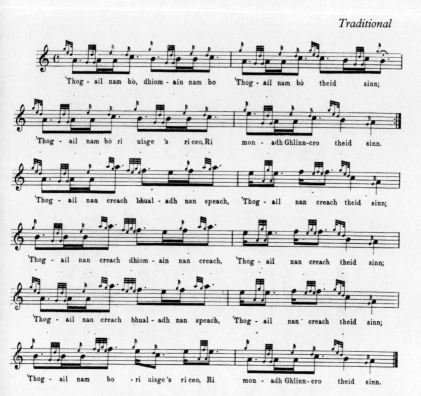